CAREER EXAMINATION SERIES

THIS IS YOUR **PASSBOOK**® FOR ...

MOTOR VEHICLE LICENSE CLERK

NATIONAL LEARNING CORPORATION®
passbooks.com

COPYRIGHT NOTICE

Copyright © 2020 by

National Learning Corporation

212 Michael Drive, Syosset, NY 11791
(516) 921-8888 • www.passbooks.com
E-mail: info@passbooks.com

PUBLISHED IN THE UNITED STATES OF AMERICA

PASSBOOK® SERIES

THE *PASSBOOK® SERIES* has been created to prepare applicants and candidates for the ultimate academic battlefield – the examination room.

At some time in our lives, each and every one of us may be required to take an examination – for validation, matriculation, admission, qualification, registration, certification, or licensure.

Based on the assumption that every applicant or candidate has met the basic formal educational standards, has taken the required number of courses, and read the necessary texts, the *PASSBOOK® SERIES* furnishes the one special preparation which may assure passing with confidence, instead of failing with insecurity. Examination questions – together with answers – are furnished as the basic vehicle for study so that the mysteries of the examination and its compounding difficulties may be eliminated or diminished by a sure method.

This book is meant to help you pass your examination provided that you qualify and are serious in your objective.

The entire field is reviewed through the huge store of content information which is succinctly presented through a provocative and challenging approach – the question-and-answer method.

A climate of success is established by furnishing the correct answers at the end of each test.

You soon learn to recognize types of questions, forms of questions, and patterns of questioning. You may even begin to anticipate expected outcomes.

You perceive that many questions are repeated or adapted so that you can gain acute insights, which may enable you to score many sure points.

You learn how to confront new questions, or types of questions, and to attack them confidently and work out the correct answers.

You note objectives and emphases, and recognize pitfalls and dangers, so that you may make positive educational adjustments.

Moreover, you are kept fully informed in relation to new concepts, methods, practices, and directions in the field.

You discover that you arre actually taking the examination all the time: you are preparing for the examination by "taking" an examination, not by reading extraneous and/or supererogatory textbooks.

In short, this PASSBOOK®, used directedly, should be an important factor in helping you to pass your test.

MOTOR VEHICLE LICENSE CLERK

DUTIES:
This position involves determining eligibility for drivers' licenses and vehicle registration through a review of the applications and a variety of supporting documents, and transmitting this information to a central computer using a computer terminal. For drivers' licenses, a check must be made of the application itself for accuracy and completeness of information, proof of age, conviction record, record of mental or physical illness and any other supporting documents that may be required. For registrations, a check must be made of the application itself for accuracy and completeness of information, proof of ownership, insurance coverage, vehicle inspection certificate, if required, and any other supporting documents. The work is performed under general supervision allowing for some leeway in the exercise of independent judgment in carrying out the details of the work. Supervision over the work of others is not a function of this position.

EXAMPLES OF TYPICAL TASKS:
Receives approved license and registration documents for processing; types and verifies data from original documents for computer input and processing; determines type or cause of malfunction or rejection response and takes appropriate action; reviews and processes applications for all types of licenses and registrations; checks supporting documents such as proof of ownership, insurance coverage, and vehicle inspection for adequacy and completeness; conducts vision, road sign, and written tests; receives, counts, and stores license plates, stickers, forms, and other supplies; assists applicants in the proper completion of forms and answers routine requests for information; requests additional data from applicant if central computer is unable to process transaction; computes fees, collects payments, and makes change; periodically reconciles transactions and money received and reports transactions by category; may perform other clerical duties. Does related work as required.

SUBJECT OF EXAMINATION:
The written test is designed to evaluate knowledge, skills and /or abilities in the following areas:
Cashiering Principles and Practices - These questions are designed to test for an understanding of such things as proper cashiering practices; terminology; and cashiering issues pertaining to currency, checks and other negotiable instruments.
Name and number checking - These questions test for the ability to distinguish between sets of words, letters, and/or numbers that are almost exactly alike. Material is usually presented in two or three columns, and you will have to determine how the entry in the first column compares with the entry in the second column and possibly the third. You will be instructed to mark your answers according to a designated code provided in the directions.
Public contact principles and practices - These questions test for knowledge of techniques used to interact with other people, to gather and present information, and to provide assistance, advice, and effective customer service in a courteous and professional manner. Questions will cover such topics as understanding and responding to people with diverse needs, perspectives, personalities, and levels of familiarity with agency operations, as well as acting in a way that both serves the public and reflects well on your agency.
Understanding and interpreting written material - These questions test for the ability to understand and interpret written material. You will be presented with brief reading passages and will be asked questions about the passages. You should base your answers to the questions only on what is presented in the passages and not on what you may happen to know about the topic.

HOW TO TAKE A TEST

I. YOU MUST PASS AN EXAMINATION

A. *WHAT EVERY CANDIDATE SHOULD KNOW*

Examination applicants often ask us for help in preparing for the written test. What can I study in advance? What kinds of questions will be asked? How will the test be given? How will the papers be graded?

As an applicant for a civil service examination, you may be wondering about some of these things. Our purpose here is to suggest effective methods of advance study and to describe civil service examinations.

Your chances for success on this examination can be increased if you know how to prepare. Those "pre-examination jitters" can be reduced if you know what to expect. You can even experience an adventure in good citizenship if you know why civil service exams are given.

B. *WHY ARE CIVIL SERVICE EXAMINATIONS GIVEN?*

Civil service examinations are important to you in two ways. As a citizen, you want public jobs filled by employees who know how to do their work. As a job seeker, you want a fair chance to compete for that job on an equal footing with other candidates. The best-known means of accomplishing this two-fold goal is the competitive examination.

Exams are widely publicized throughout the nation. They may be administered for jobs in federal, state, city, municipal, town or village governments or agencies.

Any citizen may apply, with some limitations, such as the age or residence of applicants. Your experience and education may be reviewed to see whether you meet the requirements for the particular examination. When these requirements exist, they are reasonable and applied consistently to all applicants. Thus, a competitive examination may cause you some uneasiness now, but it is your privilege and safeguard.

C. *HOW ARE CIVIL SERVICE EXAMS DEVELOPED?*

Examinations are carefully written by trained technicians who are specialists in the field known as "psychological measurement," in consultation with recognized authorities in the field of work that the test will cover. These experts recommend the subject matter areas or skills to be tested; only those knowledges or skills important to your success on the job are included. The most reliable books and source materials available are used as references. Together, the experts and technicians judge the difficulty level of the questions.

Test technicians know how to phrase questions so that the problem is clearly stated. Their ethics do not permit "trick" or "catch" questions. Questions may have been tried out on sample groups, or subjected to statistical analysis, to determine their usefulness.

Written tests are often used in combination with performance tests, ratings of training and experience, and oral interviews. All of these measures combine to form the best-known means of finding the right person for the right job.

II. HOW TO PASS THE WRITTEN TEST

A. NATURE OF THE EXAMINATION

To prepare intelligently for civil service examinations, you should know how they differ from school examinations you have taken. In school you were assigned certain definite pages to read or subjects to cover. The examination questions were quite detailed and usually emphasized memory. Civil service exams, on the other hand, try to discover your present ability to perform the duties of a position, plus your potentiality to learn these duties. In other words, a civil service exam attempts to predict how successful you will be. Questions cover such a broad area that they cannot be as minute and detailed as school exam questions.

In the public service similar kinds of work, or positions, are grouped together in one "class." This process is known as *position-classification*. All the positions in a class are paid according to the salary range for that class. One class title covers all of these positions, and they are all tested by the same examination.

B. FOUR BASIC STEPS

1) Study the announcement

How, then, can you know what subjects to study? Our best answer is: "Learn as much as possible about the class of positions for which you've applied." The exam will test the knowledge, skills and abilities needed to do the work.

Your most valuable source of information about the position you want is the official exam announcement. This announcement lists the training and experience qualifications. Check these standards and apply only if you come reasonably close to meeting them.

The brief description of the position in the examination announcement offers some clues to the subjects which will be tested. Think about the job itself. Review the duties in your mind. Can you perform them, or are there some in which you are rusty? Fill in the blank spots in your preparation.

Many jurisdictions preview the written test in the exam announcement by including a section called "Knowledge and Abilities Required," "Scope of the Examination," or some similar heading. Here you will find out specifically what fields will be tested.

2) Review your own background

Once you learn in general what the position is all about, and what you need to know to do the work, ask yourself which subjects you already know fairly well and which need improvement. You may wonder whether to concentrate on improving your strong areas or on building some background in your fields of weakness. When the announcement has specified "some knowledge" or "considerable knowledge," or has used adjectives like "beginning principles of…" or "advanced … methods," you can get a clue as to the number and difficulty of questions to be asked in any given field. More questions, and hence broader coverage, would be included for those subjects which are more important in the work. Now weigh your strengths and weaknesses against the job requirements and prepare accordingly.

3) Determine the level of the position

Another way to tell how intensively you should prepare is to understand the level of the job for which you are applying. Is it the entering level? In other words, is this the position in which beginners in a field of work are hired? Or is it an intermediate or advanced level? Sometimes this is indicated by such words as "Junior" or "Senior" in the class title. Other jurisdictions use Roman numerals to designate the level – Clerk I, Clerk II, for example. The word "Supervisor" sometimes appears in the title. If the level is not indicated by the title, check the description of duties. Will you be working under very close supervision, or will you have responsibility for independent decisions in this work?

4) Choose appropriate study materials

Now that you know the subjects to be examined and the relative amount of each subject to be covered, you can choose suitable study materials. For beginning level jobs, or even advanced ones, if you have a pronounced weakness in some aspect of your training, read a modern, standard textbook in that field. Be sure it is up to date and has general coverage. Such books are normally available at your library, and the librarian will be glad to help you locate one. For entry-level positions, questions of appropriate difficulty are chosen – neither highly advanced questions, nor those too simple. Such questions require careful thought but not advanced training.

If the position for which you are applying is technical or advanced, you will read more advanced, specialized material. If you are already familiar with the basic principles of your field, elementary textbooks would waste your time. Concentrate on advanced textbooks and technical periodicals. Think through the concepts and review difficult problems in your field.

These are all general sources. You can get more ideas on your own initiative, following these leads. For example, training manuals and publications of the government agency which employs workers in your field can be useful, particularly for technical and professional positions. A letter or visit to the government department involved may result in more specific study suggestions, and certainly will provide you with a more definite idea of the exact nature of the position you are seeking.

III. KINDS OF TESTS

Tests are used for purposes other than measuring knowledge and ability to perform specified duties. For some positions, it is equally important to test ability to make adjustments to new situations or to profit from training. In others, basic mental abilities not dependent on information are essential. Questions which test these things may not appear as pertinent to the duties of the position as those which test for knowledge and information. Yet they are often highly important parts of a fair examination. For very general questions, it is almost impossible to help you direct your study efforts. What we can do is to point out some of the more common of these general abilities needed in public service positions and describe some typical questions.

1) General information

Broad, general information has been found useful for predicting job success in some kinds of work. This is tested in a variety of ways, from vocabulary lists to questions about current events. Basic background in some field of work, such as sociology or economics, may be sampled in a group of questions. Often these are principles which have become familiar to most persons through exposure rather than through formal training. It is difficult to advise you how to study for these questions; being alert to the world around you is our best suggestion.

2) Verbal ability

An example of an ability needed in many positions is verbal or language ability. Verbal ability is, in brief, the ability to use and understand words. Vocabulary and grammar tests are typical measures of this ability. Reading comprehension or paragraph interpretation questions are common in many kinds of civil service tests. You are given a paragraph of written material and asked to find its central meaning.

3) Numerical ability

Number skills can be tested by the familiar arithmetic problem, by checking paired lists of numbers to see which are alike and which are different, or by interpreting charts and graphs. In the latter test, a graph may be printed in the test booklet which you are asked to use as the basis for answering questions.

4) Observation

A popular test for law-enforcement positions is the observation test. A picture is shown to you for several minutes, then taken away. Questions about the picture test your ability to observe both details and larger elements.

5) Following directions

In many positions in the public service, the employee must be able to carry out written instructions dependably and accurately. You may be given a chart with several columns, each column listing a variety of information. The questions require you to carry out directions involving the information given in the chart.

6) Skills and aptitudes

Performance tests effectively measure some manual skills and aptitudes. When the skill is one in which you are trained, such as typing or shorthand, you can practice. These tests are often very much like those given in business school or high school courses. For many of the other skills and aptitudes, however, no short-time preparation can be made. Skills and abilities natural to you or that you have developed throughout your lifetime are being tested.

Many of the general questions just described provide all the data needed to answer the questions and ask you to use your reasoning ability to find the answers. Your best preparation for these tests, as well as for tests of facts and ideas, is to be at your physical and mental best. You, no doubt, have your own methods of getting into an exam-taking mood and keeping "in shape." The next section lists some ideas on this subject.

IV. KINDS OF QUESTIONS

Only rarely is the "essay" question, which you answer in narrative form, used in civil service tests. Civil service tests are usually of the short-answer type. Full instructions for answering these questions will be given to you at the examination. But in case this is your first experience with short-answer questions and separate answer sheets, here is what you need to know:

1) Multiple-choice Questions

Most popular of the short-answer questions is the "multiple choice" or "best answer" question. It can be used, for example, to test for factual knowledge, ability to solve problems or judgment in meeting situations found at work.

A multiple-choice question is normally one of three types—
- It can begin with an incomplete statement followed by several possible endings. You are to find the one ending which *best* completes the statement, although some of the others may not be entirely wrong.
- It can also be a complete statement in the form of a question which is answered by choosing one of the statements listed.
- It can be in the form of a problem – again you select the best answer.

Here is an example of a multiple-choice question with a discussion which should give you some clues as to the method for choosing the right answer:

When an employee has a complaint about his assignment, the action which will *best* help him overcome his difficulty is to
- A. discuss his difficulty with his coworkers
- B. take the problem to the head of the organization
- C. take the problem to the person who gave him the assignment
- D. say nothing to anyone about his complaint

In answering this question, you should study each of the choices to find which is best. Consider choice "A" – Certainly an employee may discuss his complaint with fellow employees, but no change or improvement can result, and the complaint remains unresolved. Choice "B" is a poor choice since the head of the organization probably does not know what assignment you have been given, and taking your problem to him is known as "going over the head" of the supervisor. The supervisor, or person who made the assignment, is the person who can clarify it or correct any injustice. Choice "C" is, therefore, correct. To say nothing, as in choice "D," is unwise. Supervisors have and interest in knowing the problems employees are facing, and the employee is seeking a solution to his problem.

2) True/False Questions

The "true/false" or "right/wrong" form of question is sometimes used. Here a complete statement is given. Your job is to decide whether the statement is right or wrong.

SAMPLE: A roaming cell-phone call to a nearby city costs less than a non-roaming call to a distant city.

This statement is wrong, or false, since roaming calls are more expensive.
This is not a complete list of all possible question forms, although most of the others are variations of these common types. You will always get complete directions for

answering questions. Be sure you understand *how* to mark your answers – ask questions until you do.

V. RECORDING YOUR ANSWERS

Computer terminals are used more and more today for many different kinds of exams.

For an examination with very few applicants, you may be told to record your answers in the test booklet itself. Separate answer sheets are much more common. If this separate answer sheet is to be scored by machine – and this is often the case – it is highly important that you mark your answers correctly in order to get credit.

An electronic scoring machine is often used in civil service offices because of the speed with which papers can be scored. Machine-scored answer sheets must be marked with a pencil, which will be given to you. This pencil has a high graphite content which responds to the electronic scoring machine. As a matter of fact, stray dots may register as answers, so do not let your pencil rest on the answer sheet while you are pondering the correct answer. Also, if your pencil lead breaks or is otherwise defective, ask for another.

Since the answer sheet will be dropped in a slot in the scoring machine, be careful not to bend the corners or get the paper crumpled.

The answer sheet normally has five vertical columns of numbers, with 30 numbers to a column. These numbers correspond to the question numbers in your test booklet. After each number, going across the page are four or five pairs of dotted lines. These short dotted lines have small letters or numbers above them. The first two pairs may also have a "T" or "F" above the letters. This indicates that the first two pairs only are to be used if the questions are of the true-false type. If the questions are multiple choice, disregard the "T" and "F" and pay attention only to the small letters or numbers.

Answer your questions in the manner of the sample that follows:

32. The largest city in the United States is
    A. Washington, D.C.
    B. New York City
    C. Chicago
    D. Detroit
    E. San Francisco

1) Choose the answer you think is best. (New York City is the largest, so "B" is correct.)
2) Find the row of dotted lines numbered the same as the question you are answering. (Find row number 32)
3) Find the pair of dotted lines corresponding to the answer. (Find the pair of lines under the mark "B.")
4) Make a solid black mark between the dotted lines.

VI. BEFORE THE TEST

Common sense will help you find procedures to follow to get ready for an examination. Too many of us, however, overlook these sensible measures. Indeed, nervousness and fatigue have been found to be the most serious reasons why applicants fail to do their best on civil service tests. Here is a list of reminders:

- Begin your preparation early – Don't wait until the last minute to go scurrying around for books and materials or to find out what the position is all about.
- Prepare continuously – An hour a night for a week is better than an all-night cram session. This has been definitely established. What is more, a night a week for a month will return better dividends than crowding your study into a shorter period of time.
- Locate the place of the exam – You have been sent a notice telling you when and where to report for the examination. If the location is in a different town or otherwise unfamiliar to you, it would be well to inquire the best route and learn something about the building.
- Relax the night before the test – Allow your mind to rest. Do not study at all that night. Plan some mild recreation or diversion; then go to bed early and get a good night's sleep.
- Get up early enough to make a leisurely trip to the place for the test – This way unforeseen events, traffic snarls, unfamiliar buildings, etc. will not upset you.
- Dress comfortably – A written test is not a fashion show. You will be known by number and not by name, so wear something comfortable.
- Leave excess paraphernalia at home – Shopping bags and odd bundles will get in your way. You need bring only the items mentioned in the official notice you received; usually everything you need is provided. Do not bring reference books to the exam. They will only confuse those last minutes and be taken away from you when in the test room.
- Arrive somewhat ahead of time – If because of transportation schedules you must get there very early, bring a newspaper or magazine to take your mind off yourself while waiting.
- Locate the examination room – When you have found the proper room, you will be directed to the seat or part of the room where you will sit. Sometimes you are given a sheet of instructions to read while you are waiting. Do not fill out any forms until you are told to do so; just read them and be prepared.
- Relax and prepare to listen to the instructions
- If you have any physical problem that may keep you from doing your best, be sure to tell the test administrator. If you are sick or in poor health, you really cannot do your best on the exam. You can come back and take the test some other time.

VII. AT THE TEST

The day of the test is here and you have the test booklet in your hand. The temptation to get going is very strong. Caution! There is more to success than knowing the right answers. You must know how to identify your papers and understand variations in the type of short-answer question used in this particular examination. Follow these suggestions for maximum results from your efforts:

1) Cooperate with the monitor

The test administrator has a duty to create a situation in which you can be as much at ease as possible. He will give instructions, tell you when to begin, check to see that you are marking your answer sheet correctly, and so on. He is not there to guard you, although he will see that your competitors do not take unfair advantage. He wants to help you do your best.

2) Listen to all instructions

Don't jump the gun! Wait until you understand all directions. In most civil service tests you get more time than you need to answer the questions. So don't be in a hurry. Read each word of instructions until you clearly understand the meaning. Study the examples, listen to all announcements and follow directions. Ask questions if you do not understand what to do.

3) Identify your papers

Civil service exams are usually identified by number only. You will be assigned a number; you must not put your name on your test papers. Be sure to copy your number correctly. Since more than one exam may be given, copy your exact examination title.

4) Plan your time

Unless you are told that a test is a "speed" or "rate of work" test, speed itself is usually not important. Time enough to answer all the questions will be provided, but this does not mean that you have all day. An overall time limit has been set. Divide the total time (in minutes) by the number of questions to determine the approximate time you have for each question.

5) Do not linger over difficult questions

If you come across a difficult question, mark it with a paper clip (useful to have along) and come back to it when you have been through the booklet. One caution if you do this – be sure to skip a number on your answer sheet as well. Check often to be sure that you have not lost your place and that you are marking in the row numbered the same as the question you are answering.

6) Read the questions

Be sure you know what the question asks! Many capable people are unsuccessful because they failed to *read* the questions correctly.

7) Answer all questions

Unless you have been instructed that a penalty will be deducted for incorrect answers, it is better to guess than to omit a question.

8) Speed tests

It is often better NOT to guess on speed tests. It has been found that on timed tests people are tempted to spend the last few seconds before time is called in marking answers at random – without even reading them – in the hope of picking up a few extra points. To discourage this practice, the instructions may warn you that your score will be "corrected" for guessing. That is, a penalty will be applied. The incorrect answers will be deducted from the correct ones, or some other penalty formula will be used.

9) Review your answers

If you finish before time is called, go back to the questions you guessed or omitted to give them further thought. Review other answers if you have time.

10) Return your test materials

If you are ready to leave before others have finished or time is called, take ALL your materials to the monitor and leave quietly. Never take any test material with you. The monitor can discover whose papers are not complete, and taking a test booklet may be grounds for disqualification.

VIII. EXAMINATION TECHNIQUES

1) Read the general instructions carefully. These are usually printed on the first page of the exam booklet. As a rule, these instructions refer to the timing of the examination; the fact that you should not start work until the signal and must stop work at a signal, etc. If there are any *special* instructions, such as a choice of questions to be answered, make sure that you note this instruction carefully.

2) When you are ready to start work on the examination, that is as soon as the signal has been given, read the instructions to each question booklet, underline any key words or phrases, such as *least, best, outline, describe* and the like. In this way you will tend to answer as requested rather than discover on reviewing your paper that you *listed without describing*, that you selected the *worst* choice rather than the *best* choice, etc.

3) If the examination is of the objective or multiple-choice type – that is, each question will also give a series of possible answers: A, B, C or D, and you are called upon to select the best answer and write the letter next to that answer on your answer paper – it is advisable to start answering each question in turn. There may be anywhere from 50 to 100 such questions in the three or four hours allotted and you can see how much time would be taken if you read through all the questions before beginning to answer any. Furthermore, if you come across a question or group of questions which you know would be difficult to answer, it would undoubtedly affect your handling of all the other questions.

4) If the examination is of the essay type and contains but a few questions, it is a moot point as to whether you should read all the questions before starting to answer any one. Of course, if you are given a choice – say five out of seven and the like – then it is essential to read all the questions so you can eliminate the two that are most difficult. If, however, you are asked to answer all the questions, there may be danger in trying to answer the easiest one first because you may find that you will spend too much time on it. The best technique is to answer the first question, then proceed to the second, etc.

5) Time your answers. Before the exam begins, write down the time it started, then add the time allowed for the examination and write down the time it must be completed, then divide the time available somewhat as follows:

- If 3-1/2 hours are allowed, that would be 210 minutes. If you have 80 objective-type questions, that would be an average of 2-1/2 minutes per question. Allow yourself no more than 2 minutes per question, or a total of 160 minutes, which will permit about 50 minutes to review.
- If for the time allotment of 210 minutes there are 7 essay questions to answer, that would average about 30 minutes a question. Give yourself only 25 minutes per question so that you have about 35 minutes to review.

6) The most important instruction is to *read each question* and make sure you know what is wanted. The second most important instruction is to *time yourself properly* so that you answer every question. The third most important instruction is to *answer every question*. Guess if you have to but include something for each question. Remember that you will receive no credit for a blank and will probably receive some credit if you write something in answer to an essay question. If you guess a letter – say "B" for a multiple-choice question – you may have guessed right. If you leave a blank as an answer to a multiple-choice question, the examiners may respect your feelings but it will not add a point to your score. Some exams may penalize you for wrong answers, so in such cases *only*, you may not want to guess unless you have some basis for your answer.

7) Suggestions
   a. Objective-type questions
      1. Examine the question booklet for proper sequence of pages and questions
      2. Read all instructions carefully
      3. Skip any question which seems too difficult; return to it after all other questions have been answered
      4. Apportion your time properly; do not spend too much time on any single question or group of questions
      5. Note and underline key words – *all, most, fewest, least, best, worst, same, opposite,* etc.
      6. Pay particular attention to negatives
      7. Note unusual option, e.g., unduly long, short, complex, different or similar in content to the body of the question
      8. Observe the use of "hedging" words – *probably, may, most likely,* etc.
      9. Make sure that your answer is put next to the same number as the question
      10. Do not second-guess unless you have good reason to believe the second answer is definitely more correct
      11. Cross out original answer if you decide another answer is more accurate; do not erase until you are ready to hand your paper in
      12. Answer all questions; guess unless instructed otherwise
      13. Leave time for review

   b. Essay questions
      1. Read each question carefully
      2. Determine exactly what is wanted. Underline key words or phrases.
      3. Decide on outline or paragraph answer

4. Include many different points and elements unless asked to develop any one or two points or elements
5. Show impartiality by giving pros and cons unless directed to select one side only
6. Make and write down any assumptions you find necessary to answer the questions
7. Watch your English, grammar, punctuation and choice of words
8. Time your answers; don't crowd material

8) Answering the essay question

Most essay questions can be answered by framing the specific response around several key words or ideas. Here are a few such key words or ideas:

M's: manpower, materials, methods, money, management
P's: purpose, program, policy, plan, procedure, practice, problems, pitfalls, personnel, public relations

   a. Six basic steps in handling problems:
     1. Preliminary plan and background development
     2. Collect information, data and facts
     3. Analyze and interpret information, data and facts
     4. Analyze and develop solutions as well as make recommendations
     5. Prepare report and sell recommendations
     6. Install recommendations and follow up effectiveness

   b. Pitfalls to avoid
     1. *Taking things for granted* – A statement of the situation does not necessarily imply that each of the elements is necessarily true; for example, a complaint may be invalid and biased so that all that can be taken for granted is that a complaint has been registered
     2. *Considering only one side of a situation* – Wherever possible, indicate several alternatives and then point out the reasons you selected the best one
     3. *Failing to indicate follow up* – Whenever your answer indicates action on your part, make certain that you will take proper follow-up action to see how successful your recommendations, procedures or actions turn out to be
     4. *Taking too long in answering any single question* – Remember to time your answers properly

IX. AFTER THE TEST

Scoring procedures differ in detail among civil service jurisdictions although the general principles are the same. Whether the papers are hand-scored or graded by machine we have described, they are nearly always graded by number. That is, the person who marks the paper knows only the number – never the name – of the applicant. Not until all the papers have been graded will they be matched with names. If other tests, such as training and experience or oral interview ratings have been given, scores will be combined. Different parts of the examination usually have different weights. For example, the written test might count 60 percent of the final grade, and a rating of training and experience 40 percent. In many jurisdictions, veterans will have a certain number of points added to their grades.

After the final grade has been determined, the names are placed in grade order and an eligible list is established. There are various methods for resolving ties between those who get the same final grade – probably the most common is to place first the name of the person whose application was received first. Job offers are made from the eligible list in the order the names appear on it. You will be notified of your grade and your rank as soon as all these computations have been made. This will be done as rapidly as possible.

People who are found to meet the requirements in the announcement are called "eligibles." Their names are put on a list of eligible candidates. An eligible's chances of getting a job depend on how high he stands on this list and how fast agencies are filling jobs from the list.

When a job is to be filled from a list of eligibles, the agency asks for the names of people on the list of eligibles for that job. When the civil service commission receives this request, it sends to the agency the names of the three people highest on this list. Or, if the job to be filled has specialized requirements, the office sends the agency the names of the top three persons who meet these requirements from the general list.

The appointing officer makes a choice from among the three people whose names were sent to him. If the selected person accepts the appointment, the names of the others are put back on the list to be considered for future openings.

That is the rule in hiring from all kinds of eligible lists, whether they are for typist, carpenter, chemist, or something else. For every vacancy, the appointing officer has his choice of any one of the top three eligibles on the list. This explains why the person whose name is on top of the list sometimes does not get an appointment when some of the persons lower on the list do. If the appointing officer chooses the second or third eligible, the No. 1 eligible does not get a job at once, but stays on the list until he is appointed or the list is terminated.

X. HOW TO PASS THE INTERVIEW TEST

The examination for which you applied requires an oral interview test. You have already taken the written test and you are now being called for the interview test – the final part of the formal examination.

You may think that it is not possible to prepare for an interview test and that there are no procedures to follow during an interview. Our purpose is to point out some things you can do in advance that will help you and some good rules to follow and pitfalls to avoid while you are being interviewed.

What is an interview supposed to test?

The written examination is designed to test the technical knowledge and competence of the candidate; the oral is designed to evaluate intangible qualities, not readily measured otherwise, and to establish a list showing the relative fitness of each candidate – as measured against his competitors – for the position sought. Scoring is not on the basis of "right" and "wrong," but on a sliding scale of values ranging from "not passable" to "outstanding." As a matter of fact, it is possible to achieve a relatively low score without a single "incorrect" answer because of evident weakness in the qualities being measured.

Occasionally, an examination may consist entirely of an oral test – either an individual or a group oral. In such cases, information is sought concerning the technical knowledges and abilities of the candidate, since there has been no written examination for this purpose. More commonly, however, an oral test is used to supplement a written examination.

Who conducts interviews?

The composition of oral boards varies among different jurisdictions. In nearly all, a representative of the personnel department serves as chairman. One of the members of the board may be a representative of the department in which the candidate would work. In some cases, "outside experts" are used, and, frequently, a businessman or some other representative of the general public is asked to serve. Labor and management or other special groups may be represented. The aim is to secure the services of experts in the appropriate field.

However the board is composed, it is a good idea (and not at all improper or unethical) to ascertain in advance of the interview who the members are and what groups they represent. When you are introduced to them, you will have some idea of their backgrounds and interests, and at least you will not stutter and stammer over their names.

What should be done before the interview?

While knowledge about the board members is useful and takes some of the surprise element out of the interview, there is other preparation which is more substantive. It *is* possible to prepare for an oral interview – in several ways:

1) Keep a copy of your application and review it carefully before the interview

This may be the only document before the oral board, and the starting point of the interview. Know what education and experience you have listed there, and the sequence and dates of all of it. Sometimes the board will ask you to review the highlights of your experience for them; you should not have to hem and haw doing it.

2) Study the class specification and the examination announcement

Usually, the oral board has one or both of these to guide them. The qualities, characteristics or knowledges required by the position sought are stated in these documents. They offer valuable clues as to the nature of the oral interview. For example, if the job involves supervisory responsibilities, the announcement will usually indicate that knowledge of modern supervisory methods and the qualifications of the candidate as a supervisor will be tested. If so, you can expect such questions, frequently in the form of a hypothetical situation which you are expected to solve. NEVER go into an oral without knowledge of the duties and responsibilities of the job you seek.

3) Think through each qualification required

Try to visualize the kind of questions you would ask if you were a board member. How well could you answer them? Try especially to appraise your own knowledge and background in each area, *measured against the job sought*, and identify any areas in which you are weak. Be critical and realistic – do not flatter yourself.

4) Do some general reading in areas in which you feel you may be weak

For example, if the job involves supervision and your past experience has NOT, some general reading in supervisory methods and practices, particularly in the field of human relations, might be useful. Do NOT study agency procedures or detailed manuals. The oral board will be testing your understanding and capacity, not your memory.

5) Get a good night's sleep and watch your general health and mental attitude

You will want a clear head at the interview. Take care of a cold or any other minor ailment, and of course, no hangovers.

What should be done on the day of the interview?

Now comes the day of the interview itself. Give yourself plenty of time to get there. Plan to arrive somewhat ahead of the scheduled time, particularly if your appointment is in the fore part of the day. If a previous candidate fails to appear, the board might be ready for you a bit early. By early afternoon an oral board is almost invariably behind schedule if there are many candidates, and you may have to wait. Take along a book or magazine to read, or your application to review, but leave any extraneous material in the waiting room when you go in for your interview. In any event, relax and compose yourself.

The matter of dress is important. The board is forming impressions about you – from your experience, your manners, your attitude, and your appearance. Give your personal appearance careful attention. Dress your best, but not your flashiest. Choose conservative, appropriate clothing, and be sure it is immaculate. This is a business interview, and your appearance should indicate that you regard it as such. Besides, being well groomed and properly dressed will help boost your confidence.

Sooner or later, someone will call your name and escort you into the interview room. *This is it.* From here on you are on your own. It is too late for any more preparation. But remember, you asked for this opportunity to prove your fitness, and you are here because your request was granted.

What happens when you go in?

The usual sequence of events will be as follows: The clerk (who is often the board stenographer) will introduce you to the chairman of the oral board, who will introduce you to the other members of the board. Acknowledge the introductions before you sit down. Do not be surprised if you find a microphone facing you or a stenotypist sitting by. Oral interviews are usually recorded in the event of an appeal or other review.

Usually the chairman of the board will open the interview by reviewing the highlights of your education and work experience from your application – primarily for the benefit of the other members of the board, as well as to get the material into the record. Do not interrupt or comment unless there is an error or significant misinterpretation; if that is the case, do not hesitate. But do not quibble about insignificant matters. Also, he will usually ask you some question about your education, experience or your present job – partly to get you to start talking and to establish the interviewing "rapport." He may start the actual questioning, or turn it over to one of the other members. Frequently, each member undertakes the questioning on a particular area, one in which he is perhaps most competent, so you can expect each member to participate in the examination. Because time is limited, you may also expect some rather abrupt switches in the direction the questioning takes, so do not be upset by it. Normally, a board member will not pursue a single line of questioning unless he discovers a particular strength or weakness.

After each member has participated, the chairman will usually ask whether any member has any further questions, then will ask you if you have anything you wish to add. Unless you are expecting this question, it may floor you. Worse, it may start you off on an extended, extemporaneous speech. The board is not usually seeking more information. The question is principally to offer you a last opportunity to present further qualifications or to indicate that you have nothing to add. So, if you feel that a significant qualification or characteristic has been overlooked, it is proper to point it out in a sentence or so. Do not compliment the board on the thoroughness of their examination – they have been sketchy, and you know it. If you wish, merely say, "No thank you, I have nothing further to add." This is a point where you can "talk yourself out" of a good impression or fail to present an important bit of information. Remember, *you close the interview yourself.*

The chairman will then say, "That is all, Mr. _____, thank you." Do not be startled; the interview is over, and quicker than you think. Thank him, gather your belongings and take your leave. Save your sigh of relief for the other side of the door.

How to put your best foot forward

Throughout this entire process, you may feel that the board individually and collectively is trying to pierce your defenses, seek out your hidden weaknesses and embarrass and confuse you. Actually, this is not true. They are obliged to make an appraisal of your qualifications for the job you are seeking, and they want to see you in your best light. Remember, they must interview all candidates and a non-cooperative candidate may become a failure in spite of their best efforts to bring out his qualifications. Here are 15 suggestions that will help you:

1) Be natural – Keep your attitude confident, not cocky

If you are not confident that you can do the job, do not expect the board to be. Do not apologize for your weaknesses, try to bring out your strong points. The board is interested in a positive, not negative, presentation. Cockiness will antagonize any board member and make him wonder if you are covering up a weakness by a false show of strength.

2) Get comfortable, but don't lounge or sprawl

Sit erectly but not stiffly. A careless posture may lead the board to conclude that you are careless in other things, or at least that you are not impressed by the importance of the occasion. Either conclusion is natural, even if incorrect. Do not fuss with your clothing, a pencil or an ashtray. Your hands may occasionally be useful to emphasize a point; do not let them become a point of distraction.

3) Do not wisecrack or make small talk

This is a serious situation, and your attitude should show that you consider it as such. Further, the time of the board is limited – they do not want to waste it, and neither should you.

4) Do not exaggerate your experience or abilities

In the first place, from information in the application or other interviews and sources, the board may know more about you than you think. Secondly, you probably will not get away with it. An experienced board is rather adept at spotting such a situation, so do not take the chance.

5) If you know a board member, do not make a point of it, yet do not hide it

Certainly you are not fooling him, and probably not the other members of the board. Do not try to take advantage of your acquaintanceship – it will probably do you little good.

6) Do not dominate the interview

Let the board do that. They will give you the clues – do not assume that you have to do all the talking. Realize that the board has a number of questions to ask you, and do not try to take up all the interview time by showing off your extensive knowledge of the answer to the first one.

7) Be attentive

You only have 20 minutes or so, and you should keep your attention at its sharpest throughout. When a member is addressing a problem or question to you, give him your undivided attention. Address your reply principally to him, but do not exclude the other board members.

8) Do not interrupt

A board member may be stating a problem for you to analyze. He will ask you a question when the time comes. Let him state the problem, and wait for the question.

9) Make sure you understand the question

Do not try to answer until you are sure what the question is. If it is not clear, restate it in your own words or ask the board member to clarify it for you. However, do not haggle about minor elements.

10) Reply promptly but not hastily

A common entry on oral board rating sheets is "candidate responded readily," or "candidate hesitated in replies." Respond as promptly and quickly as you can, but do not jump to a hasty, ill-considered answer.

11) Do not be peremptory in your answers

A brief answer is proper – but do not fire your answer back. That is a losing game from your point of view. The board member can probably ask questions much faster than you can answer them.

12) Do not try to create the answer you think the board member wants

He is interested in what kind of mind you have and how it works – not in playing games. Furthermore, he can usually spot this practice and will actually grade you down on it.

13) Do not switch sides in your reply merely to agree with a board member

Frequently, a member will take a contrary position merely to draw you out and to see if you are willing and able to defend your point of view. Do not start a debate, yet do not surrender a good position. If a position is worth taking, it is worth defending.

14) Do not be afraid to admit an error in judgment if you are shown to be wrong

The board knows that you are forced to reply without any opportunity for careful consideration. Your answer may be demonstrably wrong. If so, admit it and get on with the interview.

15) Do not dwell at length on your present job

The opening question may relate to your present assignment. Answer the question but do not go into an extended discussion. You are being examined for a *new* job, not your present one. As a matter of fact, try to phrase ALL your answers in terms of the job for which you are being examined.

Basis of Rating

Probably you will forget most of these "do's" and "don'ts" when you walk into the oral interview room. Even remembering them all will not ensure you a passing grade. Perhaps you did not have the qualifications in the first place. But remembering them will help you to put your best foot forward, without treading on the toes of the board members.

Rumor and popular opinion to the contrary notwithstanding, an oral board wants you to make the best appearance possible. They know you are under pressure – but they also want to see how you respond to it as a guide to what your reaction would be under the pressures of the job you seek. They will be influenced by the degree of poise you display, the personal traits you show and the manner in which you respond.

ABOUT THIS BOOK

This book contains tests divided into Examination Sections. Go through each test, answering every question in the margin. At the end of each test look at the answer key and check your answers. On the ones you got wrong, look at the right answer choice and learn. Do not fill in the answers first. Do not memorize the questions and answers, but understand the answer and principles involved. On your test, the questions will likely be different from the samples. Questions are changed and new ones added. If you understand these past questions you should have success with any changes that arise. Tests may consist of several types of questions. We have additional books on each subject should more study be advisable or necessary for you. Finally, the more you study, the better prepared you will be. This book is intended to be the last thing you study before you walk into the examination room. Prior study of relevant texts is also recommended. NLC publishes some of these in our Fundamental Series. Knowledge and good sense are important factors in passing your exam. Good luck also helps. So now study this Passbook, absorb the material contained within and take that knowledge into the examination. Then do your best to pass that exam.

EXAMINATION SECTION

EXAMINATION SECTION
TEST 1

DIRECTIONS: Each question or incomplete statement is followed by several suggested answers or completions. Select the one that BEST answers the question or completes the statement. *PRINT THE LETTER OF THE CORRECT ANSWER IN THE SPACE AT THE RIGHT.*

1. The detection of counterfeiting and the apprehension of counterfeiters Is PRIMARILY the responsibility of the

    A. Federal Bureau of Investigation
    B. United States Secret Service
    C. Federal Reserve Board
    D. National Security Council

1.____

2. The term *legal tender* applies to

    A. a check, legally endorsed, and intended for deposit only
    B. money which may lawfully be used in the payment of debts
    C. foreign money whose rate of exchange is set by law
    D. uncoined gold or silver in the form of bullion bars

2.____

Questions 3-4.

DIRECTIONS: Questions 3 and 4 are to be answered SOLELY on the basis of the information contained in the following statement:

When a design for a new bank note of the Federal Government has been prepared by the Bureau of Engraving and Printing and has been approved by the Secretary of the Treasury, the engravers begin the work of cutting the design in steel. No one engraver does all the work. Each man is a specialist. One works only on portraits, another on lettering, another on scroll work, and so on. Each engraver, with a steel tool known as a graver, and aided by a powerful magnifying glass, carefully carves his portion of the design into the steel. He knows that one false cut or a slip of his tool, or one miscalculation of width or depth of line, may destroy the merit of his work. A single mistake means that months or weeks of labor will have been in vain. The Bureau is proud of the fact that no counterfeiter ever has duplicated the excellent work of its expert engravers.

3. According to the above statement, each engraver in the Bureau of Engraving and Printing

    A. must be approved by the Secretary of the Treasury before he can begin work on the design for a new bank note
    B. is responsible for engraving a complete design of a new bank note himself
    C. designs new bank notes and submits them for approval to the Secretary of the Treasury
    D. performs only a specific part of the work of engraving a design for a new bank note

3.____

4. According to the above statement,

4.____

A. an engraver's tools are not available to a counterfeiter
B. mistakes made in engraving a design can be corrected immediately with little delay in the work of the Bureau
C. the skilled work of the engravers has not been successfully reproduced by counter-feiters
D. careful carving and cutting by the engravers is essential to prevent damage to equipment

5. The public lays down the rules governing the type of service that it expects to be given. These rules are expressed partly in laws and partly in public opinion, which at any time may be made into law. Private business and government departments have, and always have had, the task of giving the public what it expects, a task which has lately come to be called public relations. According to the above statement,

A. government departments have the task of serving the public as it wishes to be served
B. private firms emphasize public relations more than public agencies do
C. the rules for giving the public the service it expects are all eventually made into laws
D. the task of public relations is to inform the public about the work of government departments

6. Certain personal qualities are required of an employee who is to perform a particular assignment efficiently. Since each employee possesses different qualities, experience indicates that it is important to seek and select the employee who possesses the per-sonal qualities required for the particular assignment.
According to the above statement,

A. the personal qualities of an employee should be changed to fit a particular assign-ment
B. personal qualities are more important than experience in the performance of an assignment
C. an assignment should be changed to fit the personal qualities of the employee assigned to it
D. the employee selected for an assignment should have the personal qualities needed to perform it

7. A cashier has to make many arithmetic calculations in connection with his work. Skill in arithmetic comes readily with practice; no special talent is needed.
On the basis of the above statement, it is MOST accurate to state that

A. the most important part of a cashier's job is to make calculations
B. few cashiers have the special ability needed to handle arithmetic problems easily
C. without special talent, cashiers cannot learn to do the calculations they are required to do in their work
D. a cashier can, with practice, learn to handle the computations he is required to make

8. A bonded employee is much less likely to be tempted to steal money than an unbonded   8.____
one, for he knows that a bonding company will prosecute him for the sake of principle,
whereas an employer might not ordinarily take any action against an employee if there is
no hope of recovering the stolen money.
The MOST valid implication of the above statement is that

    A. a bonded employee if often tempted to steal because he knows that his employer
is protected against the loss
    B. a bonding company will attempt to find and punish the guilty employee even when
the stolen money cannot be recovered
    C. an employer whose bonded employees do not steal is wasting the money spent to
bond them
    D. it is wasteful for a bonding company to prosecute an employee when there is no
chance of recovering the stolen money

9. The BEST of the following attitudes regarding departmental rules and regulations for a   9.____
cashier to take is that they

    A. are simply a means for justifying disciplinary action taken by a supervisor
    B. are to be interpreted by each employee as he sees fit
    C. must be obeyed even if they seem unreasonable in some cases
    D. should be read and studied but may be ignored whenever an employee feels it is
necessary to do so

10. It is MOST important for a cashier who is assigned to perform a lengthy monotonous task   10.____
to

    A. perform this task before doing his other work
    B. ask another cashier to assist him to dispose of the task quickly
    C. perform this task only when his other work has been completed
    D. take measures to prevent mistakes in performing this task

11. Although accuracy and speed are both important for a cashier in the performance of his   11.____
work, accuracy should be considered more important MAINLY because

    A. most supervisors insist on accurate work
    B. much time is lost in correcting errors
    C. a rapid rate of work cannot be maintained for any length of time
    D. speedy workers are usually inaccurate

12. Of the following, the CHIEF reason why a cashier should not be late to work in the morn-   12.____
ing is that

    A. he will probably be penalized for his lateness
    B. the work of his unit may be delayed because of his tardiness
    C. he will set a bad example for the other employees to follow
    D. a poor attendance record may affect his supervisor's evaluation of his work

13. A cashier who handles large quantities of currency should know that the term *Silver Cer-*   13.____
tificate usually referred to

    A. a receipt for silver bars deposited with a bank
    B. a form of paper money that is acceptable only for the payment of non-business
debts

    C.   a certificate issued by a refiner of silver metal to show the purity of his product

    D.   a form of paper money that is backed by silver owned by the United States Government

14.   There are 12 consecutively numbered Federal Reserve Districts, each having as its symbol a number and the corresponding letter of the alphabet. The Federal Reserve Bank in each district has the same symbol as that of its district. For example, the Federal Reserve Bank of Boston is in the first Federal Reserve District and has as its symbol the number *1* and the letter *A*. The other districts, in numerical order, are New York, Philadelphia, Cleveland, Richmond, Atlanta, Chicago, St. Louis, Minneapolis, Kansas City, Dallas, and San Francisco.

    According to the above statement, the Federal Reserve Bank of Philadelphia is represented by the   14.____

    A.   number *2* and the letter *B*

    B.   number *2* and the letter *C*

    C.   number *3* and the letter *B*

    D.   number *3* and the letter *C*

15.   Of the following, the MOST important reason for a cashier to know the portraits that appear on each denomination of paper currency is that   15.____

    A.   he will be able to count bills merely by looking at the portraits

    B.   familiarity with portraits may help him to identify a counterfeit bill that has had its denomination changed from a lower to a higher amount

    C.   a greater knowledge of currency may help increase his promotional opportunities

    D.   the United States Treasury Department sometimes changes the portraits appearing on various currency denominations

16.   The one of the following which is a characteristic of a genuine bill is that its portrait   16.____

    A.   has a fine screen of regular lines in its background

    B.   has irregular and broken lines in its background

    C.   has a very dark blue background

    D.   merges into the background

17.   Of the following characteristics, the one that is LEAST helpful in deciding whether a bill is counterfeit is that the   17.____

    A.   portrait is dull, smudgy or scratchy

    B.   serial numbers are unevenly spaced

    C.   geometric lathework is broken and indistinct

    D.   ink rubs off when the bill is rubbed on a piece of paper

18.   The color of the Treasury seal and serial number on a United States Note is always   18.____

    A.   blue   B.   gray   C.   green   D.   red

19.   The saw teeth points on the rim of the Treasury seal on a genuine bill are generally   19.____

    A.   blunt and uneven   B.   broken off and faded

    C.   indistinct   D.   sharp and evenly spaced

20. If one-half of a mutilated genuine bill is sent to the Currency Redemption Division of the Treasury Department, the bill will   20.____
    A. be redeemed at one-half of its face value
    B. be redeemed at three-fifths of its face value
    C. be redeemed at its full face value
    D. not be redeemed at all

21. The color of the Treasury seal and serial number on a Federal Reserve Note is always   21.____
    A. blue   B. brown   C. green   D. red

22. The serial number on the face of a bill is printed   22.____
    A. to the right of the portrait and to the lower left of the portrait
    B. to the left of the portrait and to the lower right of the portrait
    C. directly above the portrait and directly below the portrait
    D. in the upper left corner and the lower left corner

23. The color of the check letter on the face of a bill is always   23.____
    A. black   B. blue   C. green   D. red

24. The face plate number on the face of a bill is printed in the   24.____
    A. upper left corner   B. upper right corner
    C. lower left corner   D. lower right corner

25. If three-fifths of a mutilated genuine bill is sent to the Currency Redemption Division of the Treasury Department, the bill will   25.____
    A. be redeemed at one-half of its face value
    B. be redeemed at three-fifths of its face value
    C. be redeemed at its full face value
    D. not be redeemed at all

Questions 26 - 35.

DIRECTIONS: In Column I below are listed the names of ten men and buildings. In Column II are listed seven paper currency denominations and a category *None of the above denominations*.

In questions 26 to 35, for each man or building in Column I, print in the correspondingly numbered space on your answer sheet, the capital letter preceding the denomination in Column II on which the man or building appears. If the man or building appears on none of the listed denominations, print the letter *H* in the correspondingly numbered space on your answer sheet.

COLUMN I	COLUMN II	
26. Alexander Hamilton	A. $1	26._____
27. White House	B. $2	27._____
28. Benjamin Franklin	C. $5	28._____
29. Mount Vernon	D. $10	29._____
30. Thomas Jefferson	E. $20	30._____
31. U.S. Treasury Department	F. $50	31._____
32. Andrew Jackson	G. $100	32._____
33. United States Capitol	H. None of the above denominations	33._____
34. George Washington		34._____
35. Abraham Lincoln		35._____

———

KEY (CORRECT ANSWERS)

1.	B	11.	B	21.	C	31.	D
2.	B	12.	B	22.	A	32.	E
3.	D	13.	D	23.	A	33.	F
4.	C	14.	D	24.	D	34.	A
5.	A	15.	B	25.	C	35.	C
6.	D	16.	A	26.	D		
7.	D	17.	D	27.	E		
8.	B	18.	D	28.	G		
9.	C	19.	D	29.	H		
10.	D	20.	A	30.	B		

———

TEST 2

DIRECTIONS: Each question or incomplete statement is followed by several suggested answers or completions. Select the one that BEST answers the question or completes the statement. *PRINT THE LETTER OF THE CORRECT ANSWER IN THE SPACE AT THE RIGHT.*

1. Of the following, the characteristic which describes a genuine coin MOST accurately is that the coin usually   1.____

    A. can be bent easily at the edges
    B. can be cut easily with a knife
    C. has a bell-like ring when dropped on a hard surface
    D. will not bounce when dropped on a hard surface

2. The corrugations on the outer edge of a genuine coin are usually   2.____

    A. even and regular
    B. indistinct and blackened
    C. the same as on a counterfeit coin
    D. uneven and crooked

3. When comparing counterfeit coins with genuine ones, most counterfeit coins usually feel   3.____

    A. greasy   B. cold   C. sticky   D. damp

4. A cashier who, in the course of his duties, suffers even a minor cut should have it properly cared for so that there will be no chance for infection to set in. Amputations, and even deaths, have resulted from small neglected wounds. According to the above statement, it is MOST accurate to state that   4.____

    A. a minor cut is not usually a cause for concern
    B. minor injuries are usually worse than they seem to be
    C. minor injuries should not be neglected
    D. small wounds are more dangerous than big ones

5. Certain types of money may be photographed only with the permission of the Secretary of the Treasury. His permission is not required to photograph   5.____

    A. bills   B. bonds, bills and coins
    C. coins   D. either coins or bills

6. Sometimes in the performance of his duties, a cashier must act alone, without advice from his superior and without reference to any books or other authority for guidance. According to this statement, a cashier must, in the exercise of his duties, sometimes display   6.____

    A. sincerity   B. caution
    C. initiative   D. courtesy

7. To say that a cashier is METICULOUS in the performance of his duties is to say that he is   7.____

    A. extremely careful   B. highly enthusiastic
    C. unusually fast   D. prone to error

8. The word NEGOTIABLE as used in business transactions means MOST NEARLY   8.____

    A. valueless   B. transferable
    C. expensive   D. profitable

9. An order which is RESCINDED is   9.____

    A. cancelled   B. adopted
    C. clarified   D. misunderstood

10. The word REMUNERATION means MOST NEARLY   10.____

    A. responsibility   B. compensation
    C. complexity   D. promotional opportunity

11. Assume that you are a cashier in an agency. Of the following, the MOST important reason why you should be courteous and tactful in dealing with visitors to your agency is that   11.____

    A. some of the visitors may show their appreciation of your courtesy by writing to your supervisor commending your work
    B. visitors who are treated courteously will probably treat you in the same manner
    C. visitors who are treated discourteously may ask your superior to take disciplinary action against you
    D. it is your responsibility to give the visitors a favorable impression of the agency

12. Assume that, as a cashier, you have been assigned the task of training a new employee in the work of collecting payments from the public.
Of the following, the MOST effective technique to follow in training this employee is for you to   12.____

    A. encourage him by praising the work he has done correctly, but do not show him the mistakes he has made
    B. insist that he obey your instructions completely even if your instructions may not be clear to him
    C. encourage him to ask questions if he does not understand any of the work
    D. give him a complete understanding of his job by showing him the incorrect, as well as the correct ways of doing his work

13. Subtract the total of 9 quarters, 17 dimes and 12 nickels from the total of 6 half-dollars, 14 quarters, 8 dimes and 6 nickels.
The *answer* is   13.____

    A. $2.05   B. $3.05   C. $3.15   D. $4.15

14. A certified check is one that   14.____

    A. states the purpose for which it is drawn
    B. has funds set aside to cover it by the bank upon which it is drawn
    C. is written by the bank upon which it is drawn
    D. requires the endorsements of both the payee and the maker before it can be cashed

15. Of the following, the MOST accurate description of a cashier's check is that it   15.____

     A.   can be cashed only by the cashier of the Bank upon which it is drawn
     B.   is drawn by a bank in payment for the services of one of its cashiers
     C.   is drawn payable to the cashier of a bank by a depositor of the bank
     D.   is drawn by a bank on its own funds and signed by its cashier

16. If, on a check, the amount payable expressed in words and the amount payable   16.____
expressed in figures are not the same, then the amount payable is the

     A.   amount in figures
     B.   amount in words
     C.   average of the two amounts
     D.   lesser of the two amounts

Questions 17 - 20.

DIRECTIONS: Column I lists four different endorsements that a man named John Doe uses
to endorse checks. Column II lists the names of five types of endorsements. In
questions 17 to 20, for each endorsement listed in Column I, select the correct
name in Column II by which that endorsement is generally known.

On your answer sheet, next to the number corresponding to each type of
endorsement listed in Column I, write the capital letter preceding the name
listed in Column II by which that endorsement is generally known.

<u>COLUMN I</u>   <u>COLUMN II</u>

17.   John Doe   A.   blank   17.____

18.   Without recourse John Doe   B.   full   18.____

19.   Pay to the order of Richard Roe John Doe   C.   qualified   19.____

20.   Pay to the order of City Bank for deposit only   D.   conditional   20.____
John Doe

                                               E.   restricted

Questions 21 - 25.

DIRECTIONS: Questions 21 to 25 are based on the following table.

COLLECTIONS BY CASHIERS FOR ONE WEEK

Name of Cashier	Monday	Tuesday	Wednesday	Thursday	Friday
Adams	$7487	$7435	$8864	$9264	$9876
Baker	9687	8643	8198	7415	8714
Taylor	7403	'6035	9722	9683	9512
Moore	6869	8212	9417	8933	9463
Foster	9129	9069	7734	8121	9596

21. Of the following, the day of the week on which the MOST money was collected is   21.____

     A.   Tuesday   B.   Wednesday
     C.   Thursday   D.   Friday

22. Of the following, the day of the week on which the LEAST money was collected is   22.____

    A. Monday   B. Tuesday
    C. Wednesday   D. Friday

23. The average amount collected per day by all the cashiers is   23.____

    A. less than $42,000
    B. between $42,000 and $42,500
    C. between $42,501 and $43,000
    D. more than $43,000

24. Foster's total collection for Monday, Tuesday and Friday are greater than Taylor's total   24.____
collections for the same three days by MOST NEARLY

    A. 12%   B. 17%   C. 21%   D. 83%

25. The average amount collected per cashier on Wednesday   25.____

    A. was less than the average amount collected per cashier on Monday by $328
    B. was greater than the average amount collected per cashier on Monday by $672
    C. was less than the average amount collected per cashier on Thursday by $104
    D. was greater than the average amount collected per cashier on Thursday by $886

26. A bag contains 800 coins. Of these, 10 per cent are dimes, 30 per cent are nickels, and   26.____
the rest are quarters.
The amount of money in the bag is

    A. less than $150   B. between $150 and $300
    C. between $301 and $450   D. more than $450

27. On March 1, the revenue division of a city department counted $800,000. The money   27.____
counted on March 2 was 10 per cent less than the money counted on March 1. If the
money counted on March 3 was 10 per cent greater than the money counted on March 2,
then the money counted on March 3 was

    A. $802,000   B. $792,000
    C. $720,000   D. $700,000

28. If one cashier can count a certain sum of money in 2 hours, and another cashier can   28.____
count the same sum in 3 hours, then both cashiers working together can count this sum
in

    A. 50 minutes   B. 1 hour and 10 minutes
    C. 1 hour and 12 minutes   D. 1 hour and 20 minutes

29. If the real estate tax is $4.11 per $100 of assessed valuation, the tax on real estate   29.____
assessed at $19,500 is MOST NEARLY

    A. $47   B. $650   C. $800   D. $900

30. The tax collections in a tax office for the week ending January 11th were $468,693.80. If   30.____
this amount was 20 per cent greater than the tax collections for the week ending January
4th, the tax collections for the week ending January 4th were MOST NEARLY

    A. $328,090   B. $375,000   C. $390,580   D. $393,705

31. Assume that the real estate tax rate is $4.08 per $100 of assessed valuation. If the tax on   31.____
    a house is $1,040.40, then the assessed valuation of the house is

    A. $25,500   B. $24,000
    C. $27,000   D. $28,500

32. Cashier X receives payments from 6 taxpayers every 15 minutes. Cashier Y receives   32.____
    payments from 15 taxpayers every half-hour. If Cashier X begins work at 9 a.m., and
    Cashier Y begins work at 9:30 a.m., the time at which the two Cashiers will have
    received payments from an equal number of taxpayers is

    A. 11 a.m.   B. 11:30 a.m.   C. 12 noon   D. 12:30 p.m.

33. The real estate tax on a piece of real property in a certain city is $1,082.40. If the   33.____
    assessed valuation of the property is $26,400, then the tax rate per $100 of assessed
    valuation is

    A. less than $4.05   B. between $4.05 and $4.08
    C. between $4.09 and $4.14   D. more than $4.14

34. If $300 is invested at simple interest so as to yield a return of $18 in 9 months, the   34.____
    amount of money that must be invested at the same rate of interest so as to yield a return
    of $120 in 6 months is

    A. $3000   B. $3300   C. $2000   D. $2300

35. Mr. Smith is reconciling his bank balance on November 15th by the use of the following   35.____
    information:
    Balance as per Bank Statement, October 31st - $15,932.20 Total Checks Outstanding,
    October 31st - 1,642.29 Total Deposits, November 1st to November 15th - 715.00 Total
    Checks Drawn, November 1st to November
    15th -   1,329.63
    According to the above information, the balance that Mr. Smith's checkbook should
    show as of the close of business on November 15th is MOST NEARLY

    A. $18,290   B. $16,647
    C. $13,675   D. $12,960

KEY (CORRECT ANSWERS)

1.	C	11.	D	21.	D	31.	A
2.	A	12.	C	22.	B	32.	B
3.	A	13.	B	23.	C	33.	C
4.	C	14.	B	24.	C	34.	A
5.	C	15.	D	25.	B	35.	C
6.	C	16.	B	26.	A		
7.	A	17.	A	27.	B		
8.	B	18.	C	28.	C		
9.	A	19.	B	29.	C		
10.	B	20.	E	30.	C		

———

ADDRESS CHECKING

EXAMINATION SECTION
TEST 1

DIRECTIONS: This test is designed to measure your speed and accuracy. You are urged to work both quickly and accurately and to do correctly as many lists as you can in the time allowed. The test consists of lists of pairs of addresses. Circle the letter *A* on your answer sheet if the two addresses are exactly ALIKE in every way. Circle the letter *D* if they are DIFFERENT.

			CIRCLE CORRECT ANSWER	
1.	2134 S 20th St	2134 S 20th St	A	D
2.	4608 N Warnock St	4806 N Warnock St	A	D
3.	1202 W Girard Dr	1202 W Girard Rd	A	D
4.	3120 S Harcourt St	3120 S Harcourt St	A	D
5.	4618 W Addison St	4618 E Addison St	A	D
6.	39-B Parkway Rd	39-D Parkway Rd	A	D
7.	6425 N Delancey	6425 N Delancey	A	D
8.	5407 Columbia Rd	5407 Columbia Rd	A	D
9.	2106 Southern Ave	2106 Southern Ave	A	D
10.	Highfalls NC	Highlands NC	A	D
11.	2873 Pershing Dr	2673 Pershing Dr	A	D
12.	1329 N H Ave NW	1329 N J Ave NW	A	D
13.	13 1316 N Quinn St Arl	1316 N Quinn St Alex	A	D
14.	7507 Wyngate Dr	7505 Wyngate Dr	A	D
15.	15 2918 Colesville Rd	2918 Colesville Rd	A	D
16.	16 2071 Belvedere Dr	2071 Belvedere Dr	A	D
17.	Palmer Wash	Palmer Mich	A	D
18.	2106 16th St SW	2106 16th St SW	A	D
19.	64-23 229th St	64-23 229th St	A	D
20.	8744 E St NE	8744 E St NE	A	D
21.	668-15 Lee Dr	668-151 Lee Dr	A	D
22.	84-84 Bay 16 St	84-84 Baye 16 St	A	D
23.	1117 E Egg Lane	11117 E Egg Lane	A	D
24.	36 W Pingrey Dr Easterville Md	36 W Pingrey Dr Easterville Md	A	D
25.	A-34 N 176 Rd NE Doddsville Mich	A-34 N 176 Rd NE Doddsville Mich	A	D

KEY (CORRECT ANSWERS)

1.	A		11.	D
2.	D		12.	D
3.	D		13.	D
4.	A		14.	D
5.	D		15.	A
6.	D		16.	A
7.	A		17.	D
8.	A		18.	A
9.	A		19.	A
10.	D		20.	A

21.	D
22.	D
23.	D
24.	A
25.	A

TEST 2

This test is designed to measure your speed and accuracy. You are urged to work both quickly and accurately and to do correctly as many lists as you can in the time allowed. The test consists of lists of pairs of addresses. Circle the letter *A* on your answer sheet if the two addresses are exactly ALIKE in every way. Circle the letter *D* if they are DIFFERENT.

			CIRCLE CORRECT ANSWER	
1.	89 Mohicn Pk Ave	89 Mohcn Pk Ave	A	D
2.	355 Warburton Av	355 Waburton Av	A	D
3.	20 Otis Ave	20 Otis Av	A	D
4.	Tutle Dr Osning	Tuttle Dr Osning	A	D
5.	15 South Pl Chapqa	15 South Pl Chapqua	A	D
6.	83 McLean Ave	83 McLean Av	A	D
7.	168 Ellison Ave Bronxvil	168 Ellson Av Bronxvil	A	D
8.	77 Lvngstn Av	79 Lvngstn Ave	A	D
9.	52 1/2 Wstmnstr Dr	52 1/2 Wstmnstr Av	A	D
10.	10 132A Old Crompnd Rd	132A Old Crompond Rd	A	D
11.	581 Bway Hastgs-on-Hdsn	581 Bway Hstg-on-Hdson	A	D
12.	682 Scrsdl Rd NW	682 Scrsdl Rd NW	A	D
13.	109 S Regent Mt Ksco	109 S Regent Mt.Ksco	A	D
14.	151 N Frnch Ave Elmsfrd	151 N Frnch Ave Elmfrd	A	D
15.	12 Gomer Jefrsn Vly	12 Gomar Jefrsn Vly	A	D
16.	391 Plesnt Nw Roch	391 Plesnt NW Roch	A	D
17.	22 1/2A Keogh La	22 1/2A Keoh La	A	D
18.	159 Meetg Hse Rd Bdfrd	15 Meetg Hse Rd Bdfrd	A	D
19.	2131 Shrad Rd Brirclf Mnr	2131 Shrd Rd Brirclf Mnr	A	D
20.	139 Amackasn Ter SE	139 Amckasn Ter SE	A	D

KEY (CORRECT ANSWERS)

1.	D	11.	D
2.	D	12.	A
3.	D	13.	D
4.	D	14.	D
5.	D	15.	D
6.	D	16.	D
7.	D	17.	D
8.	D	18.	D
9.	D	19.	D
10.	D	20.	D

———

TEST 3

DIRECTIONS: This test is designed to measure your speed and accuracy. You are urged to work both quickly and accurately and to do correctly as many lists as you can in the time allowed. The test consists of lists of pairs of addresses. Circle the letter *A* on your answer sheet if the two addresses are exactly ALIKE in every way. Circle the letter *D* if they are DIFFERENT.

CIRCLE
CORRECT ANSWER

1.	429 Nthn Hale Dr Hntgtn	429 Nthn Hale Dr Htgtn	A	D
2.	111 Shubrt Dr Haupaug	111 Shubrt Dr Haupaug	A	D
3.	156 Somrs La&Indn Hd Rd	167 Somers La & Indn Hd Rd	A	D
4.	1996 Sunst Av Wsthmptn Bch	199 Sunst Av Wsthmptn Bch	A	D
5.	135 W Shincok Rd Quog	135 W Shinck Rd Quog	A	D
6.	1579 B Strght Pth Wyandnch	1579B Strght Pth Wyandich	A	D
7.	1056 Yoakm Av	1056 Yoakum Av	A	D
8.	59 Wohsepe Dr Brghtwtrs	59 Wohsepe Dr Brghtwtrs	A	D
9.	1131A Wlt Whtmn Rd	1131 Wh Whtmn Rd	A	D
10.	137 Conscnce Cir Setukt	137 Consnce Cir Setukt	A	D
11.	941 Duane Dr Lk Rnknkma	941 Duanne Dr Lk Rnknkma	A	D
12.	1896 Hustn Lndnhrst	1896 Hustn Lndnhrst	A	D
13.	187 E Islip Rd W Islip	187 E Islip Rd Islip	A	D
14.	51 Blugras La	51 Bluegras La	A	D
15.	1B Bodtch Pth Cntr Mrich	1B Bodtch Pth Centr Mrich	A	D
16.	158 Grist Ml La Halsite	158 Grist Ml La Hallsite	A	D
17.	161-35 Shendoa Blvd	161-35 Shenendoa Blvd	A	D
18.	11 Mt Sinai-Coram Rd	11 Mt Sinai-Coram Rd	A	D
19.	31-1B Old Northprt Rd & Kngs Pk Rd	31-1B Old Northprt Rd & Kngs Pk Rd	A	D
20.	867 Medfrd Ave	869 Medfrd Ave	A	D

KEY (CORRECT ANSWERS)

1.	D	11.	D
2.	A	12.	A
3.	D	13.	D
4.	D	14.	D
5.	D	15.	D
6.	D	16.	D
7.	D	17.	D
8.	A	18.	A
9.	D	19.	A
10.	D	20.	D

TEST 4

DIRECTIONS: This test is designed to measure your speed and accuracy. You are urged to work both quickly and accurately and to do correctly as many lists as you can in the time allowed. The test consists of lists of pairs of addresses. Circle the letter *A* on your answer sheet if the two addresses are exactly ALIKE in every way. Circle the letter *D* if they are DIFFERENT.

CIRCLE
CORRECT ANSWER

1.	2469 Dogwd Av E Medo	2467 Dogwd Av E Medo	A	D
2.	5613 Lakevw Av Rkvl Cntr	5613 Lakevw Av Rkv Cntr	A	D
3.	481 Shlbrn La Nw Hyd Pk	481 Shlbrn La Nw Hyd Pk	A	D
4.	246 Court Ocnsde	246 Cort Ocnsde	A	D
5.	437 Juneau Blvd Wdbry	437 Junaeu Blvd Wdbry	A	D
6.	376 Wood La Levitwn	376 Wood La Levitwn	A	D
7.	69 Aspn Flrl Pk	59 Aspn Flr Pk	A	D
8.	2835 Vilag La N Wntagh	2835 Vilage La N Wntagh	A	D
9.	3109 Devnshr Dr E Nrwch	3109 Devnshr Dr E Nrwch	A	D
10.	81-64 Yung Pl Wdmr	81-64 Young Pl Wdmr	A	D
11.	84C Muirfld Rd	84C Muirfld Rd	A	D
12.	23 Bamboola Hksvl	23 Bamboola Hksvl	A	D
13.	139D Pninsla Blvd Vly Strm	139 Pninsla Blvd Vly Strm	A	D
14.	187 Wdland Dr Plandom	187 Wdlan Dr Plandom	A	D
15.	3 Renvil Ct Mil Nk	3 Renvil Ct Ml Nk	A	D
16.	619 Cresnt Dr Old Bthpg	619 Crescnt Dr Old Bthpg	A	D
17.	1518 Unqua Rd Maspeqa	1518 Uniqua Rd Maspeqa	A	D
18.	1017 Renselr Av Atl Bch	1017 Renselr Av Atl Bch	A	D
19.	777 Brook Ct N Nw Hyd Pk	777 Brook Ct Nw Hyd Pk	A	D
20.	2016 Revre Rd Rslyn Hts	2016 Revre Rd Rsyln Hts	A	D

———

KEY (CORRECT ANSWERS)

1.	D	11.	A
2.	D	12.	A
3.	A	13.	D
4.	D	14.	D
5.	D	15.	D
6.	A	16.	D
7.	D	17.	D
8.	D	18.	A
9.	A	19.	D
10.	D	20.	D

———

TEST 5

DIRECTIONS: This test is designed to measure your speed and accuracy. You are urged to work both quickly and accurately and to do correctly as many lists as you can in the time allowed. The test consists of lists of pairs of addresses. Circle the letter *A* on your answer sheet if the two addresses are exactly ALIKE in every way. Circle the letter *D* if they are DIFFERENT.

			CIRCLE CORRECT ANSWER	
1.	2512 Pascack Rd Prms	2512 Pasack Rd Prms	A	D
2.	157 Wdlnd Dr Wdclf Lk	157 Wdlnd Dr Wdclf Lk	A	D
3.	2416A Andrsn Blvd Bgfd	2416 Andrsn Av Bgfd	A	D
4.	6215 Athlone Ter Rivr Vl	6215 Athlone Ter Rvr Vl	A	D
5.	666 Plsnt Av Up Sadl Riv	666 Plst Av Up Sadl Riv	A	D
6.	999 Elliott Pl Ruth	999 Eliott Pl Ruth	A	D
7.	357 Blauvlt Dr Hrngtn Pk	357 Blauvlt Dr Hrngtn Pk	A	D
8.	61-34 Upland Rd Ramsy	61-34 Upland Rd Rumsy	A	D
9.	1793 Arcadn Wy Plsd	179 Arcadn Wy Plsd	A	D
10.	3117 Lantna Av Engwd	3117 Lantna Av Englwd	A	D
11.	675 Spindler Ter Sd Bk	675 Spindler Ter Sd Bk	A	D
12.	546 Riverview Pl Mahwah	546 Riverview Pl Mawah	A	D
13.	3061 Hack Crist	3061 Hack Crist	A	D
14.	2099 Lemoin Ave Ft Lee	2099 Lamoin Av Ft Lee	A	D
15.	1133 Mnache Av Mmache	1133 Mnache Av Mnanche	A	D
16.	7100 Qn Ann Rd Tea	7100 Qn Ann Rd Tee	A	D
17.	1255 Euclid Ave Rdgfld Pk	1255 Euclid Av Rdgfld Pk	A	D
18.	8013 Godwin Pl Creskl	8031 Godwin Pl Creskl	A	D
19.	38-03A Alwd Pl Fr Ln	38-03A Alwd Pl Fr Ln	A	D
20.	536 Wilkes La Dmnt	536 Willkes La Dmnt	A	D

KEY (CORRECT ANSWERS)

1.	D	11.	A
2.	A	12.	D
3.	D	13.	A
4.	D	14.	D
5.	D	15.	D
6.	D	16.	D
7.	A	17.	D
8.	D	18.	D
9.	D	19.	A
10.	D	20.	D

TEST 6

DIRECTIONS: This test is designed to measure your speed and accuracy. You are urged to work both quickly and accurately and to do correctly as many lists as you can in the time allowed. The test consists of lists of pairs of addresses. Circle the letter *A* on your answer sheet if the two addresses are exactly ALIKE in every way. Circle the letter *D* if they are DIFFERENT.

CIRCLE
CORRECT ANSWER

1.	7961 Eastern Ave SE	7961 Eastern Ave SE	A	D
2.	3809 20th Rd N	3309 20th Rd N	A	D
3.	Smicksburg Pa	Smithsburg Pa	A	D
4.	Sherman Ct	Sherman Ct	A	D
5.	Richland Ga	Richland La	A	D
6.	8520 Leesburg Pike SE	8520 Leesburg Pike SE	A	D
7.	Genevia Ar	Geneva Ar	A	D
8.	104 W Jefferson St	104 W Jefferson St	A	D
9.	Meandor WV	Meander WV	A	D
10.	6327 W Mari Ct	6327 W Mari Ct	A	D
11.	3191 Draper Dr SE	3191 Draper Dr SW	A	D
12.	1415 W Green Spring Rd	1415 W Green Spring Rd	A	D
13.	Parr In	Parr In	A	D
14.	East Falmouth Ma 02536	East Falmouth Ms 02536	A	D
15.	3016 N St NW	3015 M St NW	A	D
16.	Yukon Mo	Yukon Mo	A	D
17.	7057 Brookfield Plaza	7057 Brookfield Plaza	A	D
18.	Bethel Oh 45106	Bethel Oh 45106	A	D
19.	Littleton NH	Littleton NC	A	D
20.	8909 Bowie Dr	8909 Bowie Dr	A	D

———

KEY (CORRECT ANSWERS)

1.	A		11.	D
2.	D		12.	A
3.	D		13.	A
4.	A		14.	D
5.	D		15.	D
6.	A		16.	A
7.	D		17.	A
8.	A		18.	A
9.	D		19.	D
10.	A		20.	A

TEST 7

DIRECTIONS: This test is designed to measure your speed and accuracy. You are urged to work both quickly and accurately and to do correctly as many lists as you can in the time allowed. The test consists of lists of pairs of addresses. Circle the letter *A* on your answer sheet if the two addresses are exactly ALIKE in every way. Circle the letter *D* if they are DIFFERENT.

			CIRCLE CORRECT ANSWER	
1.	Colmar Il	Colmar Il	A	D
2.	784 Matthews Dr NE	784 Matthews Dr NE	A	D
3.	2923 John Marshall Dr	2932 John Marshall Dr	A	D
4.	6023 Woodmont Rd	6023 Woodmount Rd	A	D
5.	Nolan Tx	Noland Tx	A	D
6.	342 E Lincolnia Rd	342 E Lincolnia Dr	A	D
7.	Jane Ca	Jane Ca	A	D
8.	4921 Seminary Rd	4912 Seminary Rd	A	D
9.	Ulmers SC	Ullmers SC	A	D
10.	4804 Montgomery Lane SW	48-64 Montgomery Lane SW	A	D
11.	210 E Fairfax Dr	210 W Pairfax Dr	A	D
12.	Hanapepe Hi	Hanapepe Hi	A	D
13.	450 La Calle del Punto	450 La Calle del Punto	A	D
14.	Walland Tn 37886	Walland Tn 37836	A	D
15.	Villamont Va	Villamont Va	A	D
16.	4102 Georgia Ave NW	4102 Georgia Rd NW	A	D
17.	Aroch Or	Aroch Or	A	D
18.	6531 N Walton Ave	6531 N Waldon Ave	A	D
19.	Jeff Ky	Jeff Ky	A	D
20.	Delphos la	Delphis la	A	D

———

KEY (CORRECT ANSWERS)

1.	A		11.	D
2.	A		12.	A
3.	D		13.	A
4.	D		14.	D
5.	D		15.	A
6.	D		16.	D
7.	A		17.	A
8.	D		18.	D
9.	D		19.	A
10.	A		20.	D

ADDRESS CHECKING

EXAMINATION SECTION
TEST 1

DIRECTIONS: This test is designed to measure your speed and accuracy. You are urged to work both quickly and accurately and to do correctly as many lists as you can in the time allowed. The test consists of lists of pairs of addresses. Circle the letter *A* on your answer sheet if the two addresses are exactly ALIKE in every way. Circle the letter *D* if they are DIFFERENT.

CIRCLE
CORRECT ANSWER

1.	405 Winter Rd NW	405 Winter Rd NW	A	D
2.	607 S Calaveras Rd	607 S Calaveras Rd	A	D
3.	8406 La Casa St	8406 La Cosa St	A	D
4.	121 N Rippon St	121 N Rippon St	A	D
5.	Wideman Ar	Wiseman Ar	A	D
6.	Sodus NY 14551	Sodus NY 14551	A	D
7.	3429 Hermosa Dr	3429 Hermoso Dr	A	D
8.	3628 S Zeeland St	3268 S Zeeland St	A	D
9.	1330 Cheverly Ave NE	1330 Cheverly Ave NE	A	D
10.	1689 N Derwood Dr	1689 N Derwood Dr	A	D
11.	3886 Sunrise Ct	3886 Sunrise Ct	A	D
12.	635 La Calle Mayor	653 La Calle Mayor	A	D
13.	2560 Lansford Pl	2560 Lansford St	A	D
14.	4631 Central Ave	4631 Central Ave	A	D
15.	Mason City Ia 50401	Mason City Ia 50401	A	D
16.	758 Los Arboles Ave SE	758 Los Arboles Ave SW	A	D
17.	3282 E Downington St	3282 E Dunnington St	A	D
18.	7117 N Burlingham Ave	7117 N Burlingham Ave	A	D
19.	32 Oaklawn Blvd	32 Oakland Blvd	A	D
20.	1274 Manzana Rd	1274 Manzana Rd	A	D

KEY (CORRECT ANSWERS)

1.	A	6.	A	11.	A	16.	D
2.	A	7.	D	12.	D	17.	D
3.	D	8.	D	13.	D	18.	A
4.	A	9.	A	14.	A	19.	D
5.	D	10.	A	15.	A	20.	A

———

TEST 2

DIRECTIONS: This test is designed to measure your speed and accuracy. You are urged to work both quickly and accurately and to do correctly as many lists as you can in the time allowed. The test consists of lists of pairs of addresses. Circle the letter *A* on your answer sheet if the two addresses are exactly ALIKE in every way. Circle the letter *D* if they are DIFFERENT.

			CIRCLE CORRECT ANSWER	
1.	4598 E Kenilworth Dr	4598 E Kenilworth Dr	A	D
2.	Dayton Ok 73449	Dagton Ok 73449	A	D
3.	1172 W 83rd Ave	1127 W 83rd Ave	A	D
4.	6434 E Pulaski St	6434 E Pulaski Ct	A	D
5.	2764 N Rutherford Pl	2764 N Rutherford Pl	A	D
6.	565 Greenville Blvd SW	565 Greenview Blvd SE	A	D
7.	3824 Massasoit St	3824 Massasoit St	A	D
8.	22 Sagnaw Pkwy	22 Saganaw Pkwy	A	D
9.	Byram Ct 10573	Byram Ct 10573	A	D
10.	1928 S Fairfield Ave	1928 S Fairfield St	A	D
11.	36218 Overhills Dr	36218 Overhills Dr	A	D
13.	516 Avenida de Las Americas NW	516 Avenida de Las Americas NW	A	D
14.	7526 Naraganset Pl SW	7526 Naraganset Pl SW	A	D
15.	52626 W Ogelsby Dr	52626 W Ogelsby Dr	A	D
16.	1003 Winchester Rd	1003 Westchester Rd	A	D
17.	3478 W Cavanaugh Ct	3478 W Cavenaugh Ct	A	D
18.	Kendall Ca 90551	Kendell Ca 90551	A	D
19.	225 El Camino Blvd	225 El Camino Av	A	D
20.	7310 Via de los Pisos	7310 Via de los Pinos	A	D

———

KEY (CORRECT ANSWERS)

1.	A	6.	D	11.	D	16.	D
2.	D	7.	D	12.	A	17.	D
3.	D	8.	A	13.	A	18.	D
4.	D	9.	D	14.	A	19.	D
5.	A	10.	A	15.	A	20.	D

———

TEST 3

DIRECTIONS: This test is designed to measure your speed and accuracy. You are urged to work both quickly and accurately and to do correctly as many lists as you can in the time allowed. The test consists of lists of pairs of addresses. Circle the letter *A* on your answer sheet if the two addresses are exactly ALIKE in every way. Circle the letter *D* if they are DIFFERENT.

CIRCLE
CORRECT ANSWER

1.	1987 Wellington Ave SW	1987 Wellington Ave SW	A	D
2.	3124 S 71st St	3142 S 71st St	A	D
3.	729 Lincolnwood Blvd	729 Lincolnwood Blvd	A	D
4.	1166 N Beaumont Dr	1166 S Beaumont Dr	A	D
5.	3224 W Winecona Pl	3224 W Winecona Pl	A	D
6.	608 La Calle Bienvenida	607 La Calle Bienvenida	A	D
7.	La Molte Ia 52045	La Molte Ia 52045	A	D
8.	8625 Armitage Ave NW	8625 Armitage Ave NW	A	D
9.	2343 Broadview Ave	2334 Broadview Ave	A	D
10.	4279 Sierra Grande -Ave NE	427-9 Sierra Grande Dr NE	A	D
11.	165 32d Ave	165 32d Ave	A	D
12.	12742 N Deerborn St	12724 N Deerborn St	A	D
13.	114 Estancia Ave	141 Estancia Ave	A	D
14.	351 S Berwyn Rd	351 S Berwyn Pl	A	D
15.	7732 Avenida Manana SW	7732 Avenida Manana SW	A	D
16.	6337 C St SW	6337 G St SW	A	D
17.	57895 E Drexyl Ave	58795 E Drexyl Ave	A	D
18.	Altro Tx 75923	Altra Tx 75923	A	D
19.	3465 S Nashville St	3465 N Nashville St	A	D
20.	1226 Odell Blvd NW	1226 Oddell Blvd NW	A	D

———————

KEY (CORRECT ANSWERS)

1.	A	6.	D	11.	A	16.	D
2.	D	7.	A	12.	D	17.	D
3.	A	8.	A	13.	D	18.	D
4.	D	9.	D	14.	D	19.	D
5.	A	10.	D	15.	A	20.	D

———

TEST 4

DIRECTIONS: This test is designed to measure your speed and accuracy. You are urged to work both quickly and accurately and to do correctly as many lists as you can in the time allowed. The test consists of lists of pairs of addresses. Circle the letter *A* on your answer sheet if the two addresses are exactly ALIKE in every way. Circle the letter *D* if they are DIFFERENT.

			CIRCLE CORRECT ANSWER	
1.	94002 Chappel Ct	94002 Chappel Ct	A	D
2.	512 La Vega Dr	512 La Veta Dr	A	D
3.	8774 W Winona Pl	8774 E Winona Pl	A	D
4.	6431 Ingleside St SE	6431 Ingleside St SE	A	D
5.	2270 N Leanington St	2270 N Leanington St	A	D
6.	235 Calle de Los Vecinos	235 Calle de Los Vecinos	A	D
7.	3987 E Westwood Ave	3987 W Westwood Ave	A	D
8.	Skamokawa Wa	Skamohawa Wa	A	D
9.	2674 E Champlain Cir	2764 E Champlain Cir	A	D
10.	8751 Elmhurst Blvd	8751 Elmwood Blvd	A	D
11.	6649 Solano Dr	6649 Solana Dr	A	D
12.	4423 S Escenaba St	4423 S Escenaba St	A	D
13.	1198 N St NW	1198 M St NW	A	D
14.	Sparta Ga	Sparta Va	A	D
15.	96753 Wrightwood Ave	96753 Wrightwood Ave	A	D
16.	2445 Sangamow Ave SE	2445 Sangamow Ave SE	A	D
17.	5117 E 67 Pl	5171 E 67 Pl	A	D
18.	847 Mesa Grande Pl	847 Mesa Grande Ct	A	D
19.	1100 Cermaken St	1100 Cermaker St	A	D
20.	321 Tijeras Ave NW	321 Tijeras Ave NW	A	D

KEY (CORRECT ANSWERS)

1.	A	6.	A	11.	D	16.	A
2.	D	7.	D	12.	A	17.	D
3.	D	8.	D	13.	D	18.	D
4.	A	9.	D	14.	D	19.	D
5.	A	10.	D	15.	A	20.	A

TEST 5

DIRECTIONS: This test is designed to measure your speed and accuracy. You are urged to work both quickly and accurately and to do correctly as many lists as you can in the time allowed. The test consists of lists of pairs of addresses. Circle the letter *A* on your answer sheet if the two addresses are exactly ALIKE in every way. Circle the letter *D* if they are DIFFERENT.

CIRCLE
CORRECT ANSWER

1.	3405 Prospect St	3405 Prospect St	A	D
2.	6643 Burlington Pl	6643 Burlingtown Pl	A	D
3.	851 Esperanza Blvd	851 Esperanza Blvd	A	D
4.	Jenkinjones WV	Kenkinjones W	A	D
5.	1008 Pennsylvania Ave SE	1008 Pennsylvania Ave SW	A	D
6.	2924 26th St N	2929 26th St N	A	D
7.	7115 Highland Dr	7115 Highland Dr	A	D
8.	Chaptico Md	Chaptica Md	A	D
9.	3508 Camron Mills Rd	3508 Camron Mills Rd	A	D
10.	67158 Capston Dr	67158 Capston Dr	A	D
11.	3613 S Taylor Av	3631 S Taylor Av	A	D
12.	2421 Menokin Dr	2421 Menokin Dr	A	D
13.	3226 M St NW	3226 N St NW	A	D
14.	1201 S Court House Rd	1201 S Court House Rd	A	D
15.	Findlay Ohio 45840	Findley Ohio 45840	A	D
16.	17 Bennett St	17 Bennet St	A	D
17.	7 Vine Bowl Dr	7 Vine Bowl Pl	A	D
18.	126 McKinley Av	126 MacKinley Av	A	D
19.	384 Nepperhan Rd	387 Nepperhan Rd	A	D
20.	1077 Contreras Av NW	1077 Contreras Av NW	A	D

———

KEY (CORRECT ANSWERS)

1.	A	6.	D	11.	D	16.	D
2.	D	7.	A	12.	A	17.	D
3.	A	8.	D	13.	D	18.	D
4.	D	9.	A	14.	A	19.	D
5.	D	10.	A	15.	D	20.	A

———

TEST 6

DIRECTIONS: This test is designed to measure your speed and accuracy. You are urged to work both quickly and accurately and to do correctly as many lists as you can in the time allowed. The test consists of lists of pairs of addresses. Circle the letter *A* on your answer sheet if the two addresses are exactly ALIKE in every way. Circle the letter *D* if they are DIFFERENT.

			CIRCLE CORRECT ANSWER	
1.	239 Summit Pl NE	239 Summit Pl NE	A	D
2.	152 Continental Pkwy	152 Continental Blvd	A	D
3.	8092 13th Rd S	8029 13th Rd S	A	D
4.	3906 Queensbury Rd	3906 Queensbury Rd	A	D
5.	4719 Linnean Av NW	4719 Linnean Av NE	A	D
6.	Bradford Me	Bradley Me	A	D
7.	Parrott Ga 31777	Parrott Ga 31177	A	D
8.	4312 Lowell Lane	4312 Lowell Lane	A	D
9.	6929 W 135th Place	6929 W 135th Plaza	A	D
10.	5143 Somerset Cir	5143 Somerset Cir	A	D
11.	8501 Kennedy St	8501 Kennedy St	A	D
12.	2164 E McLean Av	2164 E McLean Av	A	D
13.	7186 E St NW	7186 F St NW	A	D
14.	2121 Beechcrest Rd	2121 Beechcroft Rd	A	D
15.	324 S Alvadero St	324 S Alverado St	A	D
17.	2908 Plaza de las Estrellas	2908 Plaza de las Estrellas	A	D
18.	223 Great Falls Rd SE	223 Great Falls Dr SE	A	D
19.	Kelton SC 29354	Kelton SC 29354	A	D
20.	3201 Landover Rd	3201 Landover Rd	A	D

———

KEY (CORRECT ANSWERS)

1.	A	6.	D	11.	A	16.	D
2.	D	7.	D	12.	A	17.	A
3.	D	8.	A	13.	D	18.	D
4.	A	9.	D	14.	D	19.	A
5.	D	10.	A	15.	A	20.	A

TEST 7

DIRECTIONS: This test is designed to measure your speed and accuracy. You are urged to work both quickly and accurately and to do correctly as many lists as you can in the time allowed. The test consists of lists of pairs of addresses. Circle the letter *A* on your answer sheet if the two addresses are exactly ALIKE in every way. Circle the letter *D* if they are DIFFERENT.

CIRCLE
CORRECT ANSWER

1.	111 Caroline Pl Armnk	111 Caroline Pl Armnk	A	D
2.	21 Grnleaf Rye	121 Grnleaf Rye	A	D
3.	245 Rumsy Rd Ynkrs	245 Rumsey Rd Ynkrs	A	D
4.	927 South Peekskl	927 South Pekskl	A	D
5.	44 Monro Av Lrchmt	44 Monroe Av Lrchmt	A	D
6.	39 Andrea Ln Scrsdl	39 Andrea La Scrsdl	A	D
7.	Ruland Wy 62143	Ruland Wy 62143	A	D
8.	51 Cyprs Rd Tukaho	51 Cyprs Rd Tuckaho	A	D
9.	213 Shore Lane Rd Mahopc	213 Shore Lane Av Mahopc	A	D
10.	189 Colmbs Av Lk Oscawna	189 Columbus Av Lk Oscawna	A	D
11.	124 West Stationery Rd	124 West Stationary Rd	A	D
12.	Purdy Vt 03124	Purdy Vt 03124	A	D
13.	129 Tewksbury Rd	129 Twsksbury Rd	A	D
14.	Gallow Hill Rd SW	Gallow Hill Rd	A	D
15.	234 Myrtle Av	234 Myrtl Av	A	D
16.	35 Chase Pl NE	35 Chse Pl NE	A	D
17.	14 Terace Av	41 Terace Av	A	D
18.	Collins Pt Rd SE	Colins Pt Rd SE	A	D
19.	164 Sagmor Ct	164 Sagmor Ct	A	D
20.	117 Warburtn Dr NE	117 Wrburtn Dr NE	A	D

KEY (CORRECT ANSWERS)

1.	A	6.	D	11.	D	16.	D
2.	D	7.	A	12.	A	17.	D
3.	D	8.	D	13.	D	18.	D
4.	D	9.	D	14.	D	19.	A
5.	D	10.	D	15.	D	20.	D

———

NAME and NUMBER COMPARISONS

COMMENTARY

This test seeks to measure your ability and disposition to do a job carefully and accurately, your attention to exactness and preciseness of detail, your alertness and versatility in discerning similarities and differences between things, and your power in systematically handling written language symbols.

It is actually a test of your ability to do academic and/or clerical work, using the basic elements of verbal (qualitative) and mathematical (quantitative) learning – words and numbers.

EXAMINATION SECTION
TEST 1

Tests 1-2

DIRECTIONS: Questions 1 through 6 consist of sets of names and addresses. In each question, the name and address in Column II should be an exact copy of the name and address in Column I. *PRINT IN THE SPACE AT THE RIGHT THE LETTER:*
   A. if there is a mistake only in the name
   B. if there is a mistake only in the address
   C. if there is a mistake in both name and address
   D. if there is no mistake in either name or address

SAMPLE:

Michael Filbert   Michael Filbert
456 Reade Street   645 Reade Street
New York, N.Y. 10013   New York, N.Y. 10013

Since there is a mistake only in the address, the answer is B.

1. Esta Wong   Esta Wang   1.____
    141 West 68 St.   141 West 68 St.
    New York, N.Y. 10023   New York, N.Y. 10023

2. Dr. Alberto Grosso   Dr. Alberto Grosso   2.____
    3475 12th Avenue   3475 12th Avenue
    Brooklyn, N.Y. 11218   Brooklyn, N.Y. 11218

3. Mrs. Ruth Bortlas   Ms. Ruth Bortlas   3.____
    482 Theresa Ct.   482 Theresa Ct.
    Far Rockaway, N.Y. 11691   Far Rockaway, N.Y. 11169

4. Mr. and Mrs. Howard Fox   Mr. and Mrs. Howard Fox   4.____
    2301 Sedgwick Ave.   231 Sedgwick Ave.
    Bronx, N.Y. 10468   Bronx, N.Y. 10468

5. Miss Marjorie Black   Miss Margorie Black   5.____
    223 East 23 Street   223 East 23 Street
    New York, N.Y. 10010   New York, N.Y. 10010

6.   Michelle Herman
     806 Valley Rd.
     Old Tappan, N.J. 07675

     Michelle Hermann
     806 Valley Dr.
     Old Tappan, N.J. 07675

6.____

KEY (CORRECT ANSWERS)

1.   A
2.   D
3.   C
4.   B
5.   A
6.   C

TEST 2

Questions 1 through 6 consist of sets of names and addresses. In each question, the name and address in Column II should be an exact copy of the name and address in Column I. *PRINT IN THE SPACE AT THE RIGHT THE LETTER:*

- A. if there is a mistake only in the name
- B. if there is a mistake only in the address
- C. if there is a mistake in both name and address
- D. if there is no mistake in either name or address

	Column I	Column II	
1.	Ms. Joan Kelly 313 Franklin Ave. Brooklyn, N.Y. 11202	Ms. Joan Kielly 318 Franklin Ave. Brooklyn, N.Y. 11202	1.____
2.	Mrs. Eileen Engel 47-24 86 Road Queens, N.Y. 11122	Mrs. Ellen Engel 47-24 86 Road Queens, N.Y. 11122	2.____
3.	Marcia Michaels 213 E. 81 St. New York, N.Y. 10012	Marcia Michaels 213 E. 81 St. New York, N.Y. 10012	3.____
4.	Rev. Edward J. Smyth 1401 Brandeis Street San Francisco, Calif. 96201	Rev. Edward J. Smyth 1401 Brandies Street San Francisco, Calif. 96201	4.____
5.	Alicia Rodriguez 24-68 81 St. Elmhurst, N.Y. 11122	Alicia Rodriquez 2468 81 St. Elmhurst, N.Y. 11122	5.____
6.	Ernest Eisemann 21 Columbia St. New York, N.Y. 10007	Ernest Eisermann 21 Columbia St. New York, N.Y. 10007	6.____

___

KEY (CORRECT ANSWERS)

1. C
2. A
3. D
4. B
5. C
6. A

___

TEST 3

DIRECTIONS: Questions 1 through 8 consist of names, locations and telephone numbers. In each question, the name, location and number in Column II should be an exact copy of the name, location and number in Column I. *PRINT IN THE SPACE AT THE RIGHT THE LETTER:*

- A. if there is a mistake in one line only
- B. if there is a mistake in two lines only
- C. if there is a mistake in three lines only
- D. if there are no mistakes in any of the lines

1. Ruth Lang
    EAM Bldg., Room C101
    625-2000, ext. 765

    Ruth Lang
    EAM Bldg., Room C110
    625-2000, ext. 765   1._____

2. Anne Marie Ionozzi
    Investigations, Room 827
    576-4000, ext. 832

    Anna Marie Ionozzi
    Investigation, Room 827
    566-4000, ext. 832   2._____

3. Willard Jameson
    Fm C Bldg. Room 687
    454-3010

    Willard Jamieson
    Fm C Bldg. Room 687
    454-3010   3._____

4. Joanne Zimmermann
    Bldg. SW, Room 314
    532-4601

    Joanne Zimmermann
    Bldg. SW, Room 314
    532-4601   4._____

5. Carlyle Whetstone
    Payroll Division-A, Room 212A
    262-5000, ext. 471

    Caryle Whetstone
    Payroll Division-A, Room 212A
    262-5000, ext. 417   5._____

6. Kenneth Chiang
    Legal Council, Room 9745
    (201) 416-9100, ext. 17

    Kenneth Chiang
    Legal Counsel, Room 9745
    (201) 416-9100, ext. 17   6._____

7. Ethel Koenig
    Personnel Services Div, Rm 433
    635-7572

    Ethel Hoenig
    Personal Services Div, Rm 433
    635-7527   7._____

8. Joyce Ehrhardt
    Office of Administrator, Rm W56
    387-8706

    Joyce Ehrhart
    Office of Administrator, Rm W56
    387-7806   8._____

KEY (CORRECT ANSWERS)

1. A
2. C
3. A
4. D
5. B

6. A
7. C
8. B

———

TEST 4

DIRECTIONS: Each of questions 1 through 10 gives the identification number and name of a person who has received treatment at a certain hospital. You are to choose the option (A, B, C or D) which has EXACTLY the same number and name as those given in the question.

SAMPLE:
123765 Frank Y. Jones
- A. 123675 Frank Y. Jones
- B. 123765 Frank T. Jones
- C. 123765 Frank Y. Johns
- D. 123765 Frank Y. Jones

The correct answer is D, because it is the only option showing the identification number and name exactly as they are in the sample question.

1. 754898 Diane Malloy   1._____

- A. 745898 Diane Malloy
- B. 754898 Dion Malloy
- C. 754898 Diane Malloy
- D. 754898 Diane Maloy

2. 661818 Ferdinand Figueroa   2._____

- A. 661818 Ferdinand Figeuroa
- B. 661618 Ferdinand Figueroa
- C. 661818 Ferdnand Figueroa
- D. 661818 Ferdinand Figueroa

3. 100101 Norman D. Braustein   3._____

- A. 100101 Norman D. Braustein
- B. 101001 Norman D. Braustein
- C. 100101 Norman P. Braustien
- D. 100101 Norman D. Bruastein

4. 838696 Robert Kittredge   4._____

- A. 838969 Robert Kittredge
- B. 838696 Robert Kittredge
- C. 388696 Robert Kittredge
- D. 838696 Robert Kittridge

5. 243716 Abraham Soletsky   5._____

- A. 243716 Abrahm Soletsky
- B. 243716 Abraham Solestky
- C. 243176 Abraham Soletsky
- D. 243716 Abraham Soletsky

6. 981121 Phillip M. Maas

    A. 981121 Phillip M. Mass
    B. 981211 Phillip M. Maas
    C. 981121 Phillip M. Maas
    D. 981121 Phillip N. Maas

    6.____

7. 786556 George Macalusso

    A. 785656 George Macalusso
    B. 786556 George Macalusso
    C. 786556 George Maculusso
    D. 786556 George Macluasso

    7.____

8. 639472 Eugene Weber

    A. 639472 Eugene Weber
    B. 639472 Eugene Webre
    C. 693472 Eugene Weber
    D. 639742 Eugene Weber

    8.____

9. 724936 John J. Lomonaco

    A. 724936 John J. Lomanoco
    B. 724396 John L. Lomonaco
    C. 724936 John J. Lomonaco
    D. 724936 John J. Lamonaco

    9.____

10. 899868 Michael Schnitzer

    A. 899868 Micheal Schnitzer
    B. 898968 Michael Schnizter
    C. 899688 Michael Schnitzer
    D. 899868 Michael Schnitzer

    10.____

———

KEY (CORRECT ANSWERS)

1.	C	6.	C
2.	D	7.	B
3.	A	8.	A
4.	B	9.	C
5.	D	10.	D

———

NAME AND NUMBER CHECKING

EXAMINATION SECTION
TEST 1

DIRECTIONS: This test is designed to measure your speed/and accuracy. You are urged to work both quickly and accurately and to do correctly as many lists as you can in the time allowed. The test consists of lists of pairs of names and numbers. Count the number of IDENTICAL pairs in each list. Then, select the correct number, 1, 2, 3, 4, or 5, and indicate your choice by circling the corresponding number on your answer paper. Two sample questions are presented for your guidance, together with the correct solutions.

SAMPLE QUESTIONS   CIRCLE
CORRECT ANSWER

SAMPLE LIST A

Adelphi College - Adelphia College   1 2 3 4 5
Braxton Corp. - Braxeton Corp.
Wassaic State School - Wassaic State School
Central Islip State Hospital - Central Isllip State Hospital
Greenwich House - Greenwich House

NOTE that there are only two correct pairs - Wassaic State School and Greenwich House. Therefore, the CORRECT answer is 2.

SAMPLE LIST B
78453694   - 78453684   1 2 3 4 5
784530   - 784530
533   - 534
67845   - 67845
2368745   - 2368755

NOTE that there are only two correct pairs - 784530 and 67845. Therefore, the CORRECT answer is 2.

LIST 1

Diagnostic Clinic   - Diagnostic Clinic   1 2 3 4 5
Yorkville Health   - Yorkville Health
Meinhard Clinic   - Meinhart Clinic
Corlears Clinic   - Carlears Clinic
Tremont Diagnostic   - Tremont Diagnostic

LIST 2
73526   - 73526   1 2 3 4 5
7283627198   - 7283627198
627   - 637
728352617283   - 728352617282
6281   - 6281

CIRCLE
CORRECT ANSWER

LIST 3

		1 2 3 4 5

Jefferson Clinic   - Jeffersen Clinic

Mott Haven Center   - Mott Havan Center

Bronx Hospital   - Bronx Hospital

Montefiore Hospital   - Montifeore Hospital

Beth Isreal Hospital   - Beth Israel Hospital

LIST 4

936271826   - 936371826   1 2 3 4 5

5271   - 5291

82637192037   - 82637192037

527182   - 5271882

726354256   - 72635456

LIST 5

Trinity Hospital   - Trinity Hospital   1 2 3 4 5

Central Harlem   - Centrel Harlem

St. Luke's Hospital   - St. Lukes' Hospital

Mt.Sinai Hospital   - Mt.Sinia Hospital

N.Y.Dispensery   - N.Y.Dispensary

LIST 6

725361552637   - 725361555637   1 2 3 4 5

7526378   - 7526377

6975   - 6975

82637481028   - 82637481028

3427   - 3429

LIST 7

Misericordia Hospital   - Miseracordia Hospital   1 2 3 4 5

Lebonan Hospital   - Lebanon Hospital

Gouverneur Hospital   - Gouverner Hospital

German Polyclinic   - German Policlinic

French Hospital   - French Hospital

LIST 8

8277364933251   - 827364933351   1 2 3 4 5

63728   - 63728

367281   - 367281

62733846273   - 6273846293

62836   - 6283

LIST 9

King's County Hospital - Kings County Hospital   1 2 3 4 5

St.Johns Long Island   - St.John's Long Island

Bellevue Hospital   - Bellvue Hospital

Beth David Hospital   - Beth David Hospital

Samaritan Hospital   - Samariton Hospital

CIRCLE
CORRECT ANSWER

LIST 10

62836454	- 62836455
42738267	- 42738369
573829	- 573829
738291627874	- 738291627874
725	- 735

1 2 3 4 5

LIST 11

Bloomingdal Clinic	- Bloomingdale Clinic
Communitty Hospital	- Community Hospital
Metroplitan Hospital	- Metropoliton Hospital
Lenox Hill Hospital	- Lonex Hill Hospital
Lincoln Hospital	- Lincoln Hospital

1 2 3 4 5

LIST 12

6283364728	- 6283648
627385	- 627383
54283902	- 54283602
63354	- 63354
7283562781	- 7283562781

1 2 3 4 5

LIST 13

Sydenham Hospital	- Sydanham Hospital
Roosevalt Hospital	- Roosevelt Hospital
Vanderbilt Clinic	- Vanderbild Clinic
Women's Hospital	- Woman's Hospital
Flushing Hospital	- Flushing Hospital

1 2 3 4 5

LIST 14

62738	- 62738
727355542321	- 72735542321
263849332	- 263849332
262837	- 263837
47382912	- 47382922

1 2 3 4 5

LIST 15

Episcopal Hospital	- Episcapal Hospital
Flower Hospital	- Flouer Hospital
Stuyvesent Clinic	- Stuyvesant Clinic
Jamaica Clinic	- Jamaica Clinic
Ridgwood Clinic	- Ridgewood Clinic

1 2 3 4 5

LIST 16

628367299	- 628367399
111	- 111
118293304829	- 1182839489
4448	- 4448
333693678	- 333693678

1 2 3 4 5

LIST 17

Arietta Crane Farm	- Areitta Crane Farm	1 2 3 4 5
Bikur Chilim Home	- Bikur Chilom Home	
Burke Foundation	- Burke Foundation	
Blythedale Home	- Blythdale Home	
Campbell Cottages	- Cambell Cottages	

LIST 18

32123	- 32132	1 2 3 4 5
273893326783	- 27389326783	
473829	- 473829	
7382937	- 7383937	
362890122332	- 36289012332	

LIST 19

Caraline Rest	- Caroline Rest	1 2 3 4 5
Loreto Rest	- Loretto Rest	
Edgewater Creche	- Edgwater Creche	
Holiday Farm	- Holiday Farm	
House of St. Giles	- House of st. Giles	

LIST 20

557286777	- 55728677	1 2 3 4 5
3678902	- 3678892	
1567839	- 1567839	
7865434712	- 7865344712	
9927382	- 9927382	

LIST 21

Isabella Home	- Isabela Home	1 2 3 4 5
James A. Moore Home	- James A. More Home	
The Robin's Nest	- The Roben's Nest	
Pelham Home	- Pelam Home	
St.Eleanora's Home	- St. Eleanora's Home	

LIST 22

273648293048	- 273648293048	1 2 3 4 5
334	- 334	
7362536478	- 7362536478	
7362819273	- 7362819273	
7362	- 7363	

LIST 23

St.Pheobe's Mission	- St.Phebe's Mission	1 2 3 4 5
Seaside Home	- Seaside Home	
Speedwell Society	- Speedwell Society	
Valeria Home	- Valera Home	
Wiltwyck	- Wildwyck	

CIRCLE
CORRECT ANSWER

LIST 24

63728	- 63738
63728192736	- 63728192738
428	- 458
62738291527	- 62738291529
63728192	- 63728192

1 2 3 4 5

LIST 25

McGaffin	- McGafin
David Ardslee	- David Ardslee
Axton Supply	- Axeton Supply Co
Alice Russell	- Alice Russell
Dobson Mfg.Co.	- Dobsen Mfg. Co.

1 2 3 4 5

KEY (CORRECT ANSWERS)

1.	3		11.	1
2.	3		12.	2
3.	1		13.	1
4.	1		14.	2
5.	1		15.	1
6.	2		16.	3
7.	1		17.	1
8.	2		18.	1
9.	1		19.	1
10.	2		20.	2

21.	1
22.	4
23.	2
24.	1
25.	2

TEST 2

DIRECTIONS: This test is designed to measure your speed and accuracy. You are urged to work both quickly and accurately and to do correctly as many lists as you can in the time allowed. The test consists of lists of pairs of names and numbers. Count the number of IDENTICAL pairs in each list. Then, select the correct number, 1, 2, 3, 4, or 5, and indicate your choice by circling the corresponding number on your answer paper. Two sample questions are presented for your guidance, together with the correct solutions.

CIRCLE
CORRECT ANSWER

LIST 1

82637381028	- 82637281028	1 2 3 4 5
928	- 928	
72937281028	- 72937281028	
7362	- 7362	
927382615	- 927382615	

LIST 2

Albee Theatre	- Albee Theatre	1 2 3 4 5
Lapland Lumber Co.	- Laplund Lumber Co.	
Adelphi College	- Adelphi College	
Jones & Son Inc.	- Jones & Sons Inc.	
S.W.Ponds Co.	- S.W. Ponds Co.	

LIST 3

85345	- 85345	1 2 3 4 5
895643278	- 895643277	
726352	- 726353	
632685	- 632685	
7263524	- 7236524	

LIST 4

Eagle Library	- Eagle Library	1 2 3 4 5
Dodge Ltd.	- Dodge Co.	
Stromberg Carlson	- Stromberg Carlsen	
Clairice Ling	- Clairice Linng	
Mason Book Co.	- Matson Book Co.	

LIST 5

66273	- 66273	1 2 3 4 5
629	- 620	
7382517283	- 7382517283	
637281	- 639281	
2738261	- 2788261	

LIST 6

Robert MacColl	- Robert McColl	1 2 3 4 5
Buick Motor	- Buck Motors	
Murray Bay & Co.Ltd.	- Murray Bay Co.Ltd.	
L.T. Ltyle	- L.T, Lyttle	
A.S. Landas	- A.S. Landas	

LIST 7

627152637490	- 627152637490	1 2 3 4 5
73526189	- 73526189	
5372	- 5392	
63728142	- 63728124	
4783946	- 4783046	

LIST 8

Tyndall Burke	- Tyndell Burke	1 2 3 4 5
W. Briehl	- W, Briehl	
Burritt Publishing Co.	- Buritt Publishing Co.	
Frederick Breyer & Co.	- Frederick Breyer Co.	
Bailey Buulard	- Bailey Bullard	

LIST 9

634	- 634	1 2 3 4 5
162837	- 163837	
273892223678	- 27389223678	
527182	- 527782	
3628901223	- 3629002223	

LIST 10

Ernest Boas	- Ernest Boas	1 2 3 4 5
Rankin Barne	- Rankin Barnes	
Edward Appley	- Edward Appely	
Camel	- Camel	
Caiger Food Co.	- Caiger Food Co.	

LIST 11

6273	- 6273	1 2 3 4 5
322	- 332	
15672839	- 15672839	
63728192637	- 63728192639	
738	- 738	

LIST 12

Wells Fargo Co.	- Wells Fargo Co.	1 2 3 4 5
W.D. Brett	- W.D. Britt	
Tassco Co.	- Tassko Co.	
Republic Mills	- Republic Mill	
R.W. Burnham	- R.W. Burhnam	

CIRCLE
CORRECT ANSWER
1 2 3 4 5

LIST 13
7253529152	- 7283529152
6283	- 6383
52839102738	- 5283910238
308	- 398
82637201927	- 8263720127

LIST 14   1 2 3 4 5
Schumacker Co.	- Shumacker Co.
C.H. Caiger	- C.H. Caiger
Abraham Strauss	- Abram Straus
B.F. Boettjer	- B.F. Boettijer
Cut-Rate Store	- Cut-Rate Stores

LIST 15   1 2 3 4 5
15273826	- 15273826
72537	- 73537
726391027384	- 72639107384
637389	- 627399
725382910	- 725382910

LIST 16   1 2 3 4 5
Hixby Ltd.	- Hixby Lt'd.
S. Reiner	- S. Riener
Reynard Co.	- Reynord Co.
Esso Gassoline Co.	- Esso Gasolene Co.
Belle Brock	- Belle Brock

LIST 17   1 2 3 4 5
7245	- 7245
819263728192	- 819263728172
682537289	- 682537298
789	- 789
82936542891	- 82936542891

LIST 18   1 2 3 4 5
Joseph Cartwright	- Joseph Cartwrite
Foote Food Co.	- Foot Food Co.
Weiman & Held	- Weiman & Held
Sanderson Shoe Co.	- Sandersen Shoe Co.
A.M. Byrne	- A.N. Byrne

LIST 19   1 2 3 4 5
4738267	- 4738277
63728	- 63729
6283628901	- 6283628991
918264	- 918264
263728192037	- 2637728192073

CIRCLE
CORRECT ANSWER

LIST 20

Exray Laboratories	- Exray Labratories	1 2 3 4 5
Curley Toy Co.	- Curly Toy Co.	
J. Lauer & Cross	- J. Laeur & Cross	
Mireco Brands	- Mireco Brands	
Sandor Lorand	- Sandor Larand	

LIST 21

607	- 609	1 2 3 4 5
6405	- 6403	
976	- 996	
101267	- 101267	
2065432	- 20965432	

LIST 22

John Macy & Sons	- John Macy & Son	1 2 3 4 5
Venus Pencil Co.	- Venus Pencil Co,	
Nell McGinnis	- Nell McGinnis	
McCutcheon & Co.	- McCutcheon & Co.	
Sun-Tan Oil	- Sun-Tan Oil	

LIST 23

703345700	- 703345700	1 2 3 4 5
46754	- 466754	
3367490	- 3367490	
3379	- 3778	
47384	- 47394	

LIST 24

arthritis	- athritis	1 2 3 4 5
asthma	- asthma	
endocrene	- endocrene	
gastro-enterological	- gastrol-enteralogical	
orthopedic	- orthopedic	

LIST 25

743829432	- 743828432	1 2 3 4 5
998	- 998	
732816253902	- 732816252902	
46829	- 46830	
7439120249	- 7439210249	

KEY (CORRECT ANSWERS)

1.	4		11.	3
2.	3		12.	1
3.	2		13.	1
4.	1		14.	1
5.	2		15.	2
6.	1		16.	1
7.	2		17.	3
8.	1		18.	1
9.	1		19.	1
10.	3		20.	1

21. 1
22. 4
23. 2
24. 3
25. 1

CODING

An ingenious question-type called coding, involving elements of alphabetizing, filing, name and number comparison, and evaluative judgment and application, has currently won wide acceptance in testing circles for measuring clerical aptitude and general ability, particularly on the senior (middle) grades (levels).

While the directions for this question-type usually vary in detail, the candidate is generally asked to consider groups of names, codes, and numbers, and, then, according to a given plan, to arrange codes in alphabetic order; to arrange these in numerical sequence; to re-arrange columns of names and numbers in correct order; to espy errors in coding; to choose the correct coding arrangement in consonance with the given directions and examples, etc.

This question-type appears to have few parameters in respect to form, substance, or degree of difficulty.

Accordingly, acquaintance with, and practice in the coding question is recommended for the serious candidate.

EXAMINATION SECTION
TEST 1

DIRECTIONS: Questions 1 through 10 are to be answered on the basis of the following Code Table. In this table every letter has a corresponding code number to be punched. Each question contains three lines of letters and code numbers. In each line, the code numbers should correspond with the letters in accordance with the table.

Letter	M	X	R	T	W	A	E	Q	Z	C
Code	1	2	3	4	5	6	7	8	9	0

On some of the lines, an error exists in the coding. Compare the letters and numbers in each question carefully. If you find an error or errors on
   only *one* of the lines in the question, mark your answer A;
   any *two* lines in the question, mark your answer B;
   all *three* lines in the question, mark your answer C;
   none of the lines in the question, mark your answer D.

SAMPLE QUESTION

XAQMZMRQ	-	26819138
RAERQEX	-	3573872
TMZCMTZA	-	46901496

In the above sample, the first line is correct since each letter, as listed, has the correct corresponding code number.
In the second line, an error exists because the letter A should have the code number 6 instead of 5.
In the third line, an error exists because the letter W should have the code number 5 instead of 6.
Since there are errors in two of the three lines, your answer should be B.

1. EQRMATTR   -   78316443   1.____
   MACWXRQW   -   16052385
   XZEMCAR   -   2971063

2. CZEMRXQ   -   0971238   2.____
   XMTARET   -   2146374
   WCEARWEC   -   50863570

3. CEXAWRQZ   -   07265389   3.____
   RCRMMZQT   -   33011984
   ACMZWTEX   -   60195472

4. XRCZQZWR   -   23089953   4.____
   CMRQCAET   -   01389574
   ZXRWTECM   -   92345701

5.	AXMTRAWR	-	62134653	5._____
	EQQCZCEW	-	77809075	
	MAZQARTM	-	16086341	
6.	WRWQCTRM	-	53580431	6._____
	CXMWAERZ	-	02156739	
	RCQEWWME	-	30865517	
7.	CRMECEAX	-	03170762	7._____
	MZCTRXRQ	-	19043238	
	XXZREMEW	-	22937175	
8.	MRCXQEAX	-	13928762	8._____
	WAMZTRMZ	-	65194319	
	ECXARWXC	-	70263520	
9.	MAWXECRQ	-	16527038	9._____
	RXQEAETM	-	32876741	
	RXEWMCZQ	-	32751098	
10.	MRQZCATE	-	13890647	10._____
	WCETRXAW	-	50743625	
	CZWMCERT	-	09510734	

KEY (CORRECT ANSWERS)

1. D
2. B
3. A
4. C
5. C

6. A
7. D
8. B
9. D
10. A

TEST 2

DIRECTIONS: Questions 1 through 6 consist of three lines of code letters and numbers. The numbers on each, line should correspond with the code letters on the same line in accordance with the table below.

Code Letter	F	X	L	M	R	W	T	S	B	H
Corresponding Number	0	1	2	3	4	5	6	7	8	9

On some of the lines, an error exists in the coding. Compare the letters and numbers in each question carefully. If you find an error or errors on
only *one* of the lines in the question, mark your answer A;
any *two* lines in the question, mark your answer B;
all *three* lines in the question, mark your answer C;
none of the lines in the question, mark your answer D.

SAMPLE QUESTION

LTSXHMF   2671930
TBRWHLM   6845913
SXLBFMR   5128034

In the above sample, the first line is correct since each code letter listed has the correct corresponding number.

On the second line, an error exists because code letter L should have the number 2 instead of the number 1.

On the third line, an error exists because the code letter S should have the number 7 instead of the number 5.

Since there are errors on two of the three lines, the correct answer is B.

1. XMWBHLR   1358924   1.____
    FWSLRHX   0572491
    MTXBLTS   3618267

2. XTLSMRF   1627340   2.____
    BMHRFLT   8394026
    HLTSWRX   9267451

3. LMBSFXS   2387016   3.____
    RWLMBSX   4532871
    SMFXBHW   7301894

4. RSTWTSML   47657632   4.____
    LXRMHFBS   21439087
    FTLBMRWX   06273451

5. XSRSBWFM   17478603   5.____
    BRMXRMXT   84314216
    XSTFBWRL   17609542

6.   TMSBXHLS   63781927   6._____
     RBSFLFWM   48702053
     MHFXWTRS   39015647

KEY (CORRECT ANSWERS)

1.   D
2.   A
3.   C
4.   B
5.   C
6.   D

TEST 3

DIRECTIONS: Questions 1 through 5 consist of three lines of code letters and numbers. The numbers on each line should correspond with the code letters on the same line in accordance with the table below.

Code Letter	P	L	I	J	B	O	H	U	C	G
Corresponding Number	0	1	2	3	4	5	6	7	8	9

On some of the lines, an error exists in the coding. Compare the letters and numbers in each question carefully. If you find an error or errors on

only *one* of the lines in the question, mark your answer A;
any *two* lines in the question, mark your answer B;
all *three* lines in the question, mark your answer C;
none of the lines in the question, mark your answer D.

SAMPLE QUESTION

JHOILCP   3652180
BICLGUP   4286970
UCIBHLJ   5824613

In the above sample, the first line is correct since each code letter listed has the correct corresponding number.
On the second line, an error exists because code letter L should have the number 1 instead of the number 6.
On the third line an error exists because the code letter U should have the number 7 instead of the number 5.
Since there are errors on two of the three lines, the correct answer is B.

1. BULJCIP   4713920   1. _____
    HIGPOUL   6290571
    OCUHJBI   5876342

2. CUBLOIJ   8741023   2. _____
    LCLGCLB   1818914
    JPUHIOC   3076158

3. OIJGCBPO   52398405   3. _____
    UHPBLIOP   76041250
    CLUIPGPC   81720908

4. BPCOUOJI   40875732   4. _____
    UOHCIPLB   75682014
    GLHUUCBJ   92677843

5. HOIOHJLH   65256361   5. _____
    IOJJHHBP   25536640
    OJHBJOPI   53642502

KEY (CORRECT ANSWERS)

1. A
2. C
3. D
4. B
5. C

TEST 4

DIRECTIONS: Questions 1 through 5 consist of three lines of code letters and numbers. The numbers on each line should correspond with the code letters on the same line in accordance with the table below.

Code Letters	Q	S	L	Y	M	O	U	N	W	Z
Corresponding Numbers	1	2	3	4	5	6	7	8	9	0

On some of the lines, an error exists in the coding. Compare the letters and numbers in each question carefully. If you find an error on

only *one* of the lines in the question, mark your answer A;
any *two* lines in the question, mark your answer B;
all *three* lines in the question, mark your answer C;
none of the lines in the question, mark your answer D.

SAMPLE QUESTION
MOQNWZQS   56189012
QWNMOLYU   19865347
LONLMYWN   36835489

In the above sample, the first line is correct since each code letter, as listed, has the correct corresponding number.
On the second line, an error exists because code letter M should have the number 5 instead of the number 6.
On the third line an error exists because the code letter W should have the number 9 instead of the number 8.
Since there are errors on two of the three lines, the correct answer is B.

1. SMUWOLQN   25796318   1.____
   ULSQNMZL   73218503
   NMYQZUSL   85410723

2. YUWWMYQZ   47995410   2.____
   SOSOSQSO   26262126
   ZUNLWMYW   07839549

3. QULSWZYN   17329045   3.____
   ZYLQWOYF   04319639
   QLUYWZSO   13749026

4. NLQZOYUM   83106475   4.____
   SQMUWZOM   21579065
   MMYWMZSQ   55498021

5. NQLOWZZU   81319007   5.____
   SMYLUNZO   25347806
   UWMSNZOL   79528013

KEY (CORRECT ANSWERS)

1. D
2. D
3. B
4. A
5. C

TEST 5

DIRECTIONS: Answer Questions 1 through 6 *SOLELY* on the basis of the chart and the instructions given below.

Toll Rate	$.25	$.30	$.45	$.60	$.75	$8.90	$1.20	$2.50
Classification Number of Vehicle	1	2	3	4	5	6	7	8

Assume that each of the amounts of money on the above chart is a toll rate charged for a type of vehicle and that the number immediately below each amount is the classification number for that type of vehicle. For instance, "1" is the classification number for a vehicle paying a $.25 toll; "2" is the classification number for a vehicle paying a $.30 toll; and so forth.

In each question, a series of tolls is given in Column I. Column II gives four different arrangements of classification numbers. You are to pick the answer (A, B, C, or D) in Column II that gives the classification numbers that match the tolls in Column I and are in the same order as the tolls in Column I.

SAMPLE QUESTION

	Column I				Column II			
$.30,	$.90,	$2.50,	$.45	A.	2,	6,	8,	2
				B.	2,	8,	6,	3
				C.	2,	6,	8,	3
				D.	1,	6,	8,	3

According to the chart, the classification numbers that correspond to these toll rates are as follows: $.30 - 2, $.90 - 6, $2.50 - 8, $.45 -3. Therefore, the right answer is 2, 6, 8, 3. The answer is C in Column II.

Do the following questions in the same way.

Column I   Column II

1. $.60, $.30, $.90, $1.20, $.60

    A. 4, 6, 2, 8, 4
    B. 4, 2, 6, 7, 4
    C. 2, 4, 7, 6, 2
    D. 2, 4, 6, 7, 4

1._____

2. $.90, $.45, $.25, $.45, $2.50, $.75

    A. 6, 3, 1, 3, 8, 3
    B. 6, 3, 3, 1, 8, 5
    C. 6, 1, 3, 3, 8, 5
    D. 6, 3, 1, 3, 8, 5

2._____

3. $.45, $.75, $1.20, $.25, $.25, $.30, $.45

    A. 3, 5, 7, 1, 1, 2, 3
    B. 5, 3, 7, 1, 1, 2, 3
    C. 3, 5, 7, 1, 2, 1, 3
    D. 3, 7, 5, 1, 1, 2, 3

3._____

4. $1.20, $2.50, $.45, $.90, $1.20, $.75, $.25

    A. 7, 8, 5, 6, 7, 5, 1
    B. 7, 8, 3, 7, 6, 5, 1
    C. 7, 8, 3, 6, 7, 5, 1
    D. 7, 8, 3, 6, 7, 1, 5

4._____

5. $2.50, $1.20, $.90, $.25, $.60, $.45, $.30

    A. 8, 6, 7, 1, 4, 3, 2
    B. 8, 7, 5, 1, 4, 3, 2
    C. 8, 7, 6, 2, 4, 3, 2
    D. 8, 7, 6, 1, 4, 3, 2

5.____

6. $.75, $.25, $.45, $.60, $.90, $.30, $2.50

    A. 5, 1, 3, 2, 4, 6, 8
    B. 5, 1, 3, 4, 2, 6, 8
    C. 5, 1, 3, 4, 6, 2, 8
    D. 5, 3, 1, 4, 6, 2, 8

6.____

KEY (CORRECT ANSWERS)

1. B
2. D
3. A
4. C
5. D
6. C

TEST 6

DIRECTIONS: Answer Questions 1 through 10 on the basis of the following information:
A code number for any item is obtained by combining the date of delivery, number of units received, and number of units used. The first two digits represent the day of the month, the third and fourth digits represent the month, and the fifth and sixth digits represent the year.
The number following the letter R represents the number of units received and the number following the letter U represents the number of units used.
For example, the code number 120603-R5690-U1001 indicates that a delivery of 5,690 units was made on June 12, 2003 of which 1,001 units were used.

Questions 1-6.

DIRECTIONS: Using the chart below, answer Questions 1 through 6 by choosing the letter (A, B, C, or D) in which the supplier and stock number correspond to the code number given.

Supplier	Stock Number	Number of Units Received	Delivery Date	Number of Units Used
Stony	38390	8300	May 11, 2002	3800
Stoney	39803	1780	September 15, 2003	1703
Nievo	21220	5527	October 10, 2003	5007
Nieve	38903	1733	August 5, 2003	1703
Monte	39213	5527	October 10, 2002	5007
Stony	38890	3308	December 9, 2002	3300
Stony	83930	3880	September 12, 2002	380
Nevo	47101	485	June 11, 2002	231
Nievo	12122	5725	May 11, 2003	5201
Neve	47101	9721	August 15, 2003	8207
Nievo	21120	2275	January 7, 2002	2175
Rosa	41210	3821	March 3, 2003	2710
Stony	38890	3308	September 12, 2002	3300
Dinal	54921	1711	April 2, 2003	1117
Stony	33890	8038	March 5, 2003	3300
Dinal	54721	1171	March 2, 2002	717
Claridge	81927	3308	April 5, 2003	3088
Nievo	21122	4878	June 7, 2002	3492
Haley	39670	8300	December 23, 2003	5300

1. Code No. 120902-R3308-U3300   1.____

   A. Nievo - 12122   B. Stony - 83930
   C. Nievo - 21220   D. Stony -38890

2. Code No. 101002-R5527-U5007   2.____

   A. Nievo - 21220   B. Haley - 39670
   C. Monte - 39213   D. Claridge - 81927

3. Code No. 101003-R5527-U5007   3.____

   A. Nievo - 21220   B. Monte - 39213
   C. Nievo - 12122   D. Nievo - 21120

4. Code No. 110503-R5725-U5201   4._____

    A. Nievo - 12122   B. Nievo - 21220
    C. Haley - 39670   D. Stony - 38390

5. Code No. 070102-R2275-U2175   5._____

    A. Stony - 33890   B. Stony - 83930
    C. Stony - 38390   D. Nievo - 21120

6. Code No. 120902-R3880-U380   6._____

    A. Stony - 83930   B. Stony - 38890
    C. Stony - 33890   D. Monte - 39213

Questions 7-10.

DIRECTIONS: Using the same chart, answer Questions 7 through 10 by choosing the letter (A, B, C, or D) in which the code number corresponds to the supplier and stock number given.

7. Nieve - 38903   7._____

    A. 851903-R1733-U1703   B. 080502-R1733-U1703
    C. 080503-R1733-U1703   D. 050803-R1733-U1703

8. Nevo - 47101   8._____

    A. 081503-R9721-U8207   B. 091503-R9721-U8207
    C. 110602-R485-U231   D. 061102-R485-U231

9. Dinal - 54921   9._____

    A. 020403-R1711-U1117   B. 030202-R1171-U717
    C. 020302-R1171-U717   D. 421903-R1711-U1117

10. Nievo - 21122   10._____

    A. 070602-R4878-U3492   B. 060702-R4878-U349
    C. 761902-R4878-U3492   D. 060702-R4878-U3492

KEY (CORRECT ANSWERS)

1. D
2. C
3. A
4. A
5. D

6. A
7. D
8. C
9. A
10. A

CLERICAL ABILITIES TEST

Clerical aptitude involves the ability to perceive pertinent detail in verbal or tabular material, to observe differences in copy, to proofread words and numbers, and to avoid perceptual errors in arithmetic computation.

NATURE OF THE TEST

Four types of clerical aptitude questions are presented in the Clerical Abilities Test. There are 120 questions with a short time limit. The test contains 30 questions on name and number checking, 30 on the arrangement of names in correct alphabetical order, 30 on simple arithmetic, and 30 on inspecting groups of letters and numbers. The questions have been arranged in groups or cycles of five questions of each type. The Clerical Abilities Test is primarily a test of speed in carrying out relatively simple clerical tasks. While accuracy on these tasks is important and will be taken into account in the scoring, experience has shown that many persons are so concerned about accuracy that they do the test more slowly than they should. Competitors should be cautioned that speed as well as accuracy is important to achieve a good score.

HOW THE TEST IS ADMINISTERED

Each competitor should be given a copy of the test booklet with sample questions on the cover page, an answer sheet, and a medium No. 2 pencil. Ten minutes are allowed to study the directions and sample questions and to answer the questions in the proper boxes on the two pages.

The separate answer sheet should be used for the test proper. Fifteen minutes are allowed for the test.

HOW THE TEST IS SCORED

The correct answers should be counted and recorded. The number of incorrect answers must also be counted because one-fourth of the number of incorrect answers is subtracted from the number of right answers. An omission is considered as neither a right nor a wrong answer. The score on this test is the number of right answers minus one-fourth of the number of wrong answers (fractions of one-half or less are dropped). For example, if an applicant had answered 89 questions correctly and 10 questions incorrectly, and had omitted 1 question, his score would be 87.

EXAMINATION SECTION

DIRECTIONS: This test contains four kinds of questions. There are some of each kind on each page in the booklet. The time limit for the test will be announced by the examiner.

Use the special pencil furnished by the examiner in marking your answers on the separate answer sheet. For each question, there are five suggested answers. Decide which answer is correct, find the number of the question on the answer sheet, and make a *solid black mark* between the dotted lines just below the letter of your answer. If you wish to change your answer, erase the first mark completelydo not merely cross it out.

SAMPLE QUESTIONS

In each line across the page there are three names or numbers that are much alike. Compare the three names or numbers and decide which ones are exactly alike. On the Sample Answer Sheet at the right, mark the answer-

A   if ALL THREE names or numbers are exactly ALIKE
B   if only the FIRST and SECOND names or numbers are exactly ALIKE
C   if only the FIRST and THIRD names or numbers are exactly ALIKE
D   if only the SECOND and THIRD names or numbers are exactly ALIKE
E   if ALL THREE names or numbers are DIFFERENT

I.	Davis Hazen	David Hozen	David Hazen
II.	Lois Appel	Lois Appel	Lois Apfel
III.	June Allan	Jane Allan	Jane Allan
IV.	10235	10235	10235
V.	32614	32164	32614

It will be to your advantage to learn what A, B, C, D, and E stand for. If you finish the sample questions before you are told to turn to the test, study them.

SAMPLE ANSWER SHEET

	A	B	C	D	E
I					
II					
III					
IV					
V					
VI					
VII					

In the next group of sample questions, there is a name in a box at the left, and four other names in alphabetical order at the right. Find the correct space for the boxed name so that it will be in alphabetical order with the others, and mark the letter of that space as your answer.

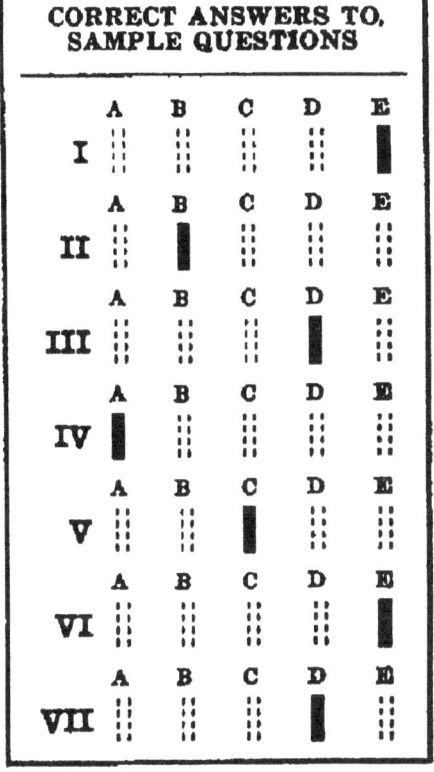

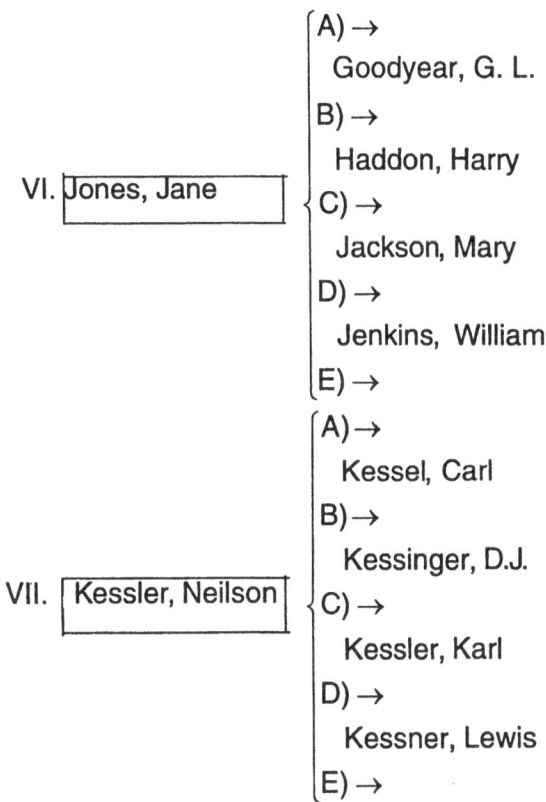

VI. Jones, Jane

A) →
　Goodyear, G. L.
B) →
　Haddon, Harry
C) →
　Jackson, Mary
D) →
　Jenkins, William
E) →

VII. Kessler, Neilson

A) →
　Kessel, Carl
B) →
　Kessinger, D.J.
C) →
　Kessler, Karl
D) →
　Kessner, Lewis
E) →

DIRECTIONS: In the following questions, complete the equation and find your answer among the list of suggested answers. Mark the Sample Answer Sheet A, B, C or D for the answer you obtained; or if your answer is not among these, mark E for that question.

VIII. Add:

   22   A) 44 B) 45
+ 33   C) 54 D) 55
          E) none of these

IX. Subtract:

   24   A) 20 B) 21
− 3   C) 27 D) 29
          E) none of these

X. Multiply:

   25   A) 100 B) 115
x 5   C) 125 D) 135
          E) none of these

XI. Divide:

          A) 20 B) 22
6 / 126 C) 24 D) 26
          E) none of these

4

Directions: There is one set of suggested answers for the next group of sample questions. Do not try to memorize these answers, because there will be a different set on each page in the test.

To find the answer to a question, find which suggested answer contains numbers and letters all of which appear in the question. If no suggested answer fits, mark E for that question.

XII. 8NK9GT46
XIII. T97Z6L3K
XIV. Z7GK398N
XV. 3K946GZL
XVI. ZN738KT9

Suggested Answers
$\begin{cases} A = 7,9,G,K \\ B = 8,9,T,Z \\ C = 6,7,K,Z \\ D = 6,8,G,T \\ E = \text{none of these} \end{cases}$

	SAMPLE ANSWER SHEET	CORRECT ANSWERS TO SAMPLE QUESTIONS
VIII	A B C D E	A B C **D** E
IX	A B C D E	A **B** C D E
X	A B C D E	A B **C** D E
XI	A B C D E	A B C D **E**
XII	A B C D E	A B C **D** E
XIII	A B C D E	A **B** C D E
XIV	A B C D E	**A** B C D E
XV	A B C D E	A B C D **E**
XVI	A B C D E	**A** B C D E

After you have marked your answers to all the questions on the Sample Answer Sheets on this page and on the front page of the booklet, check them with the answers in the boxes marked Correct Answers to Sample Questions.

In questions 1 through 5, compare the three names or numbers, and mark

A   if ALL THREE names or numbers are exactly ALIKE
B   if only the FIRST and SECOND names or numbers are exactly ALIKE
C   if only the FIRST and THIRD names or numbers are exactly ALIKE
D   if only the SECOND and THIRD names or numbers are exactly ALIKE
E   if ALL THREE names or numbers are DIFFERENT

1. 5261383   5261383   5261338
2. 8125690   8126690   8125609
3. W. E. Johnston   W. E. Johnson   W. E. Johnson
4. Vergil L. Muller Vergil L. Muller Vergil L. Muller
5. Atherton R. Warde Asheton R. Warde Atherton P. Warde

In questions 6 through 10, find the correct place for the name in the box.

6. | Hackett, Gerald |

A) →
Habert, James
B) →
Hachett, J. J.
C) →
Hachetts, K, Larson
D) →
Hachettson, Leroy
E) →

7. | Margenroth, Alvin |

A) →
Margeroth, Albert
B) →
Margestein, Dan
C) →
Margestein, David
D) →
Margue, Edgar
E) →

8. | Bobbitt, Olivier E. |

A) →
Bobbitt, D. Olivier
B) →
Bobbitt, Olive B.
C) →
Bobbitt, Olivia H.
D) →
Bobbitt, R. Olivia
E) →

9. | Mosely, Werner |

A) →
Mosely, Albert J.
B) →
Mosley, Alvin
C) →
Mosley, S. M.
D) →
Mozley, Vinson N.
E) →

10. | Youmuns, Frank L. |

A) →
Youmons, Frank G.
B) →
Youmons, Frank H.
C) →
Youmons, Frank K.
D) →
Youmons, Frank M.
E) →

GO ON TO THE NEXT COLUMN.

Answers

11. Add:
$$\begin{array}{r} 4\ 3 \\ +\ 3\ 2 \\ \hline \end{array}$$
A) 55   B) 65
C) **66**   D) 75
E) none of these

12. Subtract:
$$\begin{array}{r} 8\ 3 \\ -\ 4 \\ \hline \end{array}$$
A) 73   B) 79
C) 80   D) 89
E) none of these

13. Multiply:
$$\begin{array}{r} 4\ 1 \\ \times\ 7 \\ \hline \end{array}$$
A) 281   B) 287
C) 291   D) 297
E) none of these

14. Divide:
$$6\ \overline{)\ 3\ 0\ 6}$$
A) 44   B) 51
C) 52   D) 60
E) none of these

15. Add:
$$\begin{array}{r} 3\ 7 \\ +\ 1\ 5 \\ \hline \end{array}$$
A) 42   B) 52
C) 53   D) 62
E) none of these

For each question below, find which one of the suggested answers appears in that question.

16.   6 2 5 K 4 P T G

17.   L 4 7 2 T 6 V K

18.   3 5 4 L 9 V T G

19.   G 4 K 7 L 3 5 Z

20.   4 K 2 9 N 5 T G

Suggested Answers
A = 4, 5, K, T
B = 4, 7, G, K
C = 2, 5, G, L
D = 2, 7, L, T
E = none of these

GO ON TO THE NEXT PAGE.

In questions 21 through 25, compare the three names or numbers, and mark the answer

A   if ALL THREE names or numbers are exactly ALIKE
B   if only the FIRST and SECOND names or numbers are exactly ALIKE
C   if only the FIRST and THIRD names or numbers are exactly ALIKE
D   if only the SECOND and THIRD names or numbers are exactly ALIKE
E   if ALL THREE names or numbers are DIFFERENT

21.	2395890	2395890	2395890
22.	1926341	1926347	1926314
23.	E. Owens McVey	E. Owen McVey	E. Owen McVay
24.	Emily Neal Rouse	Emily Neal Rowse	Emily Neal Rowse
25.	H. Merritt Audubon	H. Merriott Audubon	H. Merritt Audubon

In questions 26 through 30, find the correct place for the name in the box.

26. | Watters, N. O. |

A) →
Waters, Charles L.
B) →
Waterson, Nina P.
C) →
Watson, Nora J.
D) →
Wattwood, Paul A.
E) →

27. | Johnston, Edward |

A) →
Johnston, Edgar R.
B) →
Johnston, Edmond
C) →
Johnston, Edmund
D) →
Johnstone, Edmund A.
E) →

28. | Rensch, Adeline |

A) →
Ramsay, Amos
B) →
Remschel, Augusta
C) →
Renshaw, Austin
D) →
Rentzel, Becky
E) →

29. | Schnyder, Maurice |

A) →
Schneider, Martin
B) →
Schneider, Mertens
C) →
Schnyder, Newman
D) →
Schreibner, Norman
E) →

30. | Freedenburg, C. Erma |

A) →
Freedenberg, Emerson
B) →
Freedenberg, Erma
C) →
Freedenberg, Erma E.
D) →
Freedinberg, Erma F.
E) →

GO ON TO THE NEXT COLUMN.

Answers

→ 31. Subtract:
6 8
− 4 7
——
A) 10   B) 11
C) 20   D) 22
E) none of these

32. Multiply:
5 0
× 8
——
A) 400   B) 408
C) 450   D) 458
E) none of these

33. Divide:
9 / 1 8 0
A) 20   B) 29
C) 30   D) 39
E) none of these

34. Add:
7 8
+ 6 3
——
A) 131   B) 140
C) 141   D) 151
E) none of these

35. Subtract:
8 9
− 7 0
——
A) 9   B) 18
C) 19   D) 29
E) none of these

For each question below, find which one of the suggested answers appears in that question.

36. 9 G Z 3 L 4 6 N

37. L 5 N K 4 3 9 V

38. 8 2 V P 9 L Z 5

39. V P 9 Z 5 L 8 7

40. 5 T 8 N 2 9 V L

Suggested Answers
A = 4, 9, L, V
B = 4, 5, N, Z
C = 5, 8, L, Z
D = 8, 9, N, V
E = none of these

GO ON TO THE NEXT PAGE.

In questions 41 through 45, compare the three names or numbers, and mark the answer

A   if ALL THREE names or numbers are exactly ALIKE
B   if only the FIRST and SECOND names or numbers are exactly ALIKE
C   if only the FIRST and THIRD names or numbers are exactly ALIKE
D   if only the SECOND and THIRD names or numbers are exactly ALIKE
E   if ALL THREE names or numbers are DIFFERENT

41. 6219354	6219354	6219354
42. 2312793	2312793	2312793
43. 1065407	1065407	1065047
44. Francis Ransdell	Frances Ramsdell	Francis Ramsdell
45. Cornelius Detwiler	Cornelius Detwiler	Cornelius Detwiler

In questions 46 through 50, find the correct place for the name in the box.

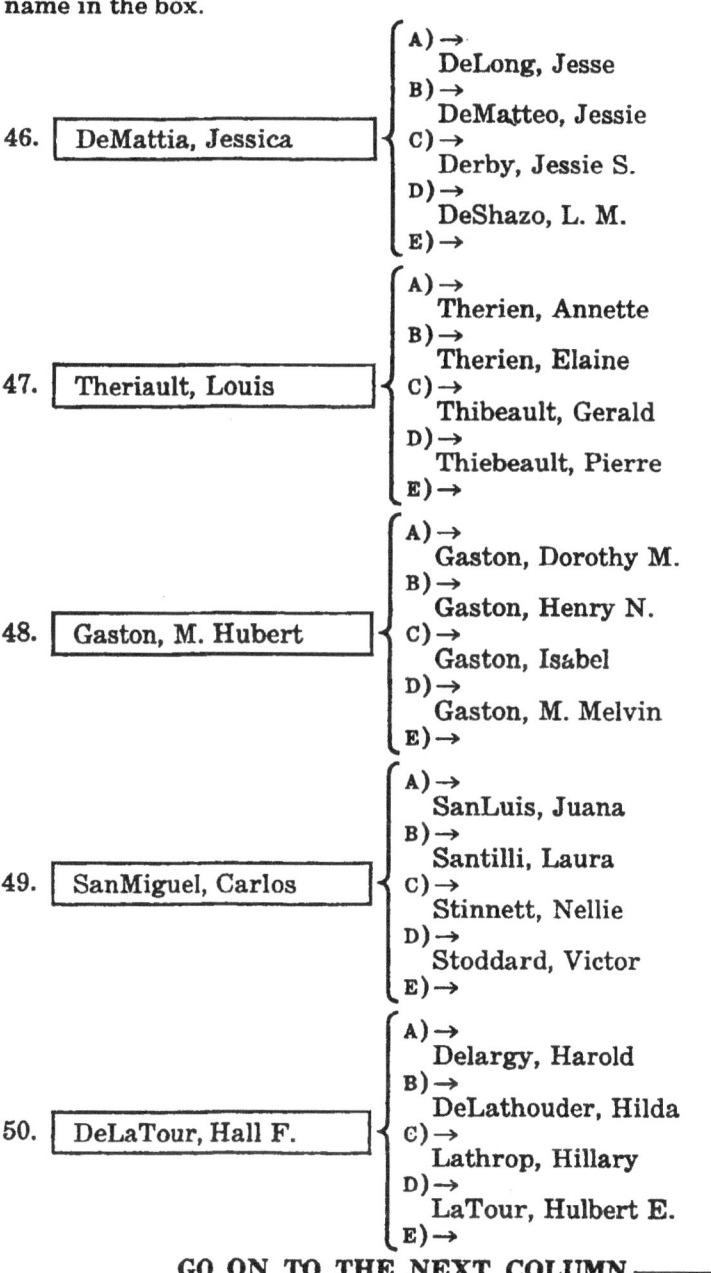

46. DeMattia, Jessica

A) →
DeLong, Jesse
B) →
DeMatteo, Jessie
C) →
Derby, Jessie S.
D) →
DeShazo, L. M.
E) →

47. Theriault, Louis

A) →
Therien, Annette
B) →
Therien, Elaine
C) →
Thibeault, Gerald
D) →
Thiebeault, Pierre
E) →

48. Gaston, M. Hubert

A) →
Gaston, Dorothy M.
B) →
Gaston, Henry N.
C) →
Gaston, Isabel
D) →
Gaston, M. Melvin
E) →

49. SanMiguel, Carlos

A) →
SanLuis, Juana
B) →
Santilli, Laura
C) →
Stinnett, Nellie
D) →
Stoddard, Victor
E) →

50. DeLaTour, Hall F.

A) →
Delargy, Harold
B) →
DeLathouder, Hilda
C) →
Lathrop, Hillary
D) →
LaTour, Hulbert E.
E) →

GO ON TO THE NEXT COLUMN.

Answers

51. Multiply:
  6 2
× 5
  ———

A) 300   B) 310
C) 315   D) 360
E) none of these

52. Divide:

3 / 1 5 3

A) 41   B) 43
C) 51   D) 53
E) none of these

53. Add:
  4 7
+ 2 1
  ———

A) 58   B) 59
C) 67   D) 68
E) none of these

54. Subtract:
  8 7
− 4 2
  ———

A) 34   B) 35
C) 44   D) 45
E) none of these

55. Multiply:
  3 7
× 3
  ———

A) 91   B) 101
C) 104   D) 114
E) none of these

For each question below, find which one of the suggested answers appears in that question.

56. N 5 4 7 T K 3 Z

57. 8 5 3 V L 2 Z N

58. 7 2 5 N 9 K L V

59. 9 8 L 2 5 Z K V

60. Z 6 5 V 9 3 P N

Suggested
Answers
A = 3, 8, K, N
B = 5, 8, N, V
C = 3, 9, V, Z
D = 5, 9, K, Z
E = none of these

GO ON TO THE NEXT PAGE.

In questions 61 through 65, compare the three names or numbers, and mark the answer

    A   if ALL THREE names or numbers are exactly ALIKE
    B   if only the FIRST and SECOND names or numbers are exactly ALIKE
    C   if only the FIRST and THIRD names or numbers are exactly ALIKE
    D   if only the SECOND and THIRD names or numbers are exactly ALIKE
    E   if ALL THREE names or numbers are DIFFERENT

61.	6452054	6452654	6452054
62.	8501268	8501268	8501286
63.	Ella Burk Newham	Ella Burk Newnham	Elena Burk Newnham
64.	Jno. K. Ravencroft	Jno. H. Ravencroft	Jno. H. Ravencoft
65.	Martin Wills Pullen	Martin Wills Pulen	Martin Wills Pullen

In questions 66 through 70, find the correct place for the name in the box.

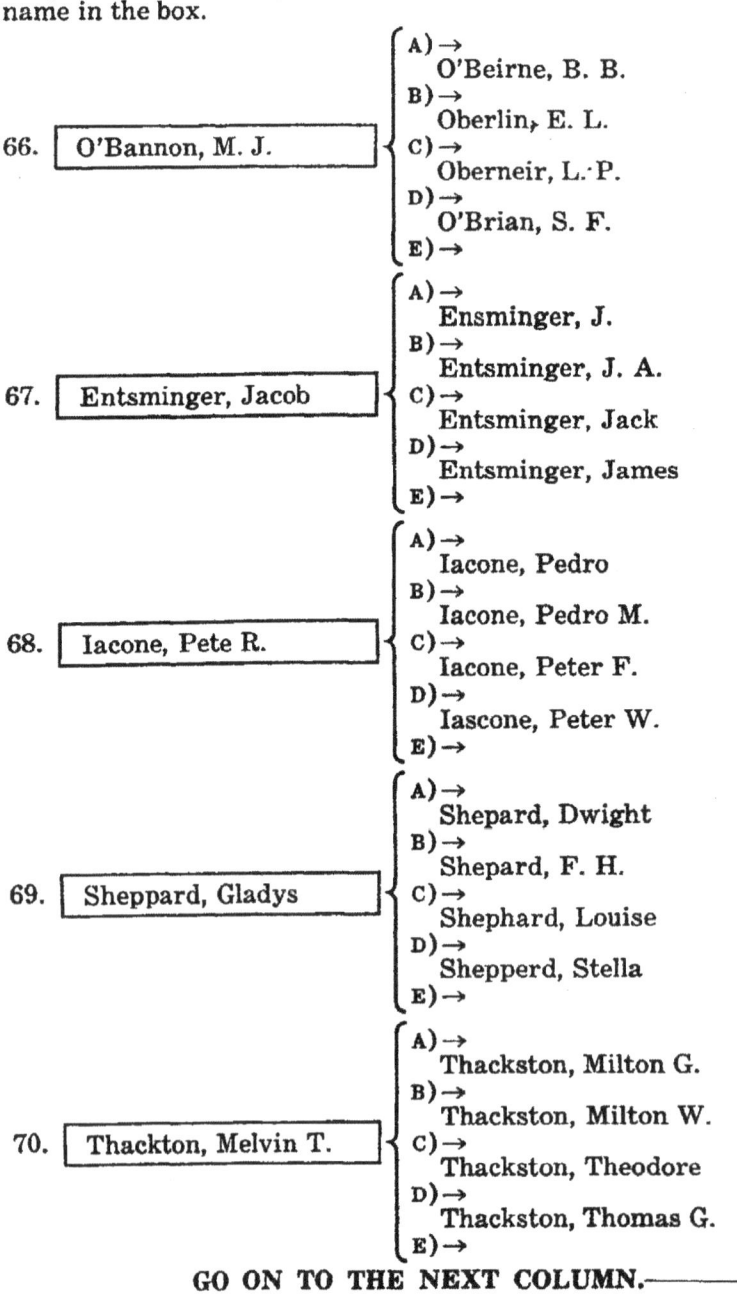

66. O'Bannon, M. J.
    A) → O'Beirne, B. B.
    B) → Oberlin, E. L.
    C) → Oberneir, L. P.
    D) → O'Brian, S. F.
    E) →

67. Entsminger, Jacob
    A) → Ensminger, J.
    B) → Entsminger, J. A.
    C) → Entsminger, Jack
    D) → Entsminger, James
    E) →

68. Iacone, Pete R.
    A) → Iacone, Pedro
    B) → Iacone, Pedro M.
    C) → Iacone, Peter F.
    D) → Iascone, Peter W.
    E) →

69. Sheppard, Gladys
    A) → Shepard, Dwight
    B) → Shepard, F. H.
    C) → Shephard, Louise
    D) → Shepperd, Stella
    E) →

70. Thackton, Melvin T.
    A) → Thackston, Milton G.
    B) → Thackston, Milton W.
    C) → Thackston, Theodore
    D) → Thackston, Thomas G.
    E) →

GO ON TO THE NEXT COLUMN.

Answers

71. Divide:

    7 / 3 5 7

    A) 51   B) 52
    C) 53   D) 54
    E) none of these

72. Add:

    5 8
   + 2 7

    A) 75   B) 84
    C) 85   D) 95
    E) none of these

73. Subtract:

    8 6
   − 5 7

    A) 18   B) 29
    C) 38   D) 39
    E) none of these

74. Multiply:

    6 8
  ×   4

    A) 242   B) 264
    C) 272   D) 274
    E) none of these

75. Divide:

    9 / 6 3 9

    A) 71   B) 73
    C) 81   D) 83
    E) none of these

For each question below, find which one of the suggested answers appears in that question.

76. 6 Z T N 8 7 4 V

77. V 7 8 6 N 5 P L

78. N 7 P V 8 4 2 L

79. 7 8 G 4 3 V L T

80. 4 8 G 2 T N 6 L

Suggested Answers
    A = 2, 7, L, N
    B = 2, 8, T, V
    C = 6, 8, L, T
    D = 6, 7, N, V
    E = none of these

GO ON TO THE NEXT PAGE.

In questions 81 through 85, compare the three names or numbers, and mark the answer

A if ALL THREE names or numbers are exactly ALIKE
B if only the FIRST and SECOND names or numbers are exactly ALIKE
C if only the FIRST and THIRD names or numbers are exactly ALIKE
D if only the SECOND and THIRD names or numbers are exactly ALIKE
E if ALL THREE names or numbers are DIFFERENT

81. 3457988	3457986	3457986
82. 4695682	4695862	4695682
83. Stricklund Kanedy	Stricklund Kanedy	Stricklund Kanedy
84. Joy Harlor Witner	Joy Harloe Witner	Joy Harloe Witner
85. R. M. O. Uberroth	R. M. O. Uberroth	R. N. O. Uberroth

In questions 86 through 90, find the correct place for the name in the box.

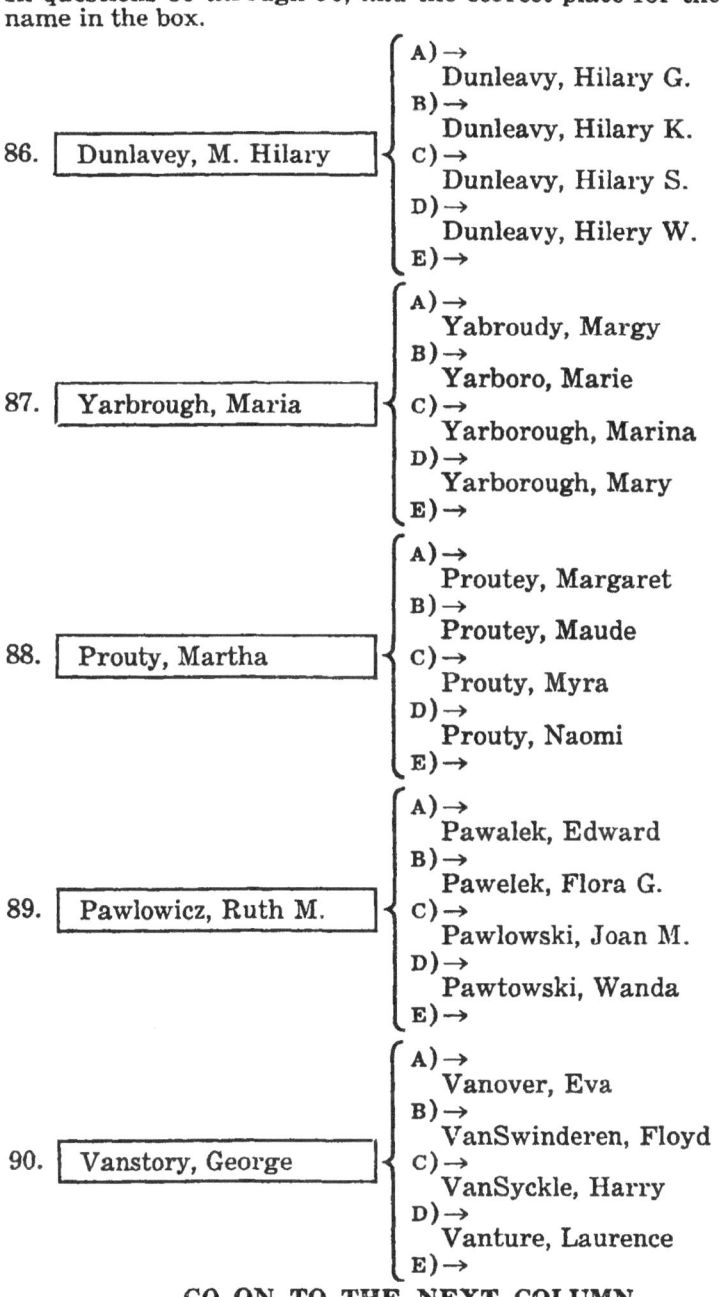

86. Dunlavey, M. Hilary
A) →
Dunleavy, Hilary G.
B) →
Dunleavy, Hilary K.
C) →
Dunleavy, Hilary S.
D) →
Dunleavy, Hilery W.
E) →

87. Yarbrough, Maria
A) →
Yabroudy, Margy
B) →
Yarboro, Marie
C) →
Yarborough, Marina
D) →
Yarborough, Mary
E) →

88. Prouty, Martha
A) →
Proutey, Margaret
B) →
Proutey, Maude
C) →
Prouty, Myra
D) →
Prouty, Naomi
E) →

89. Pawlowicz, Ruth M.
A) →
Pawalek, Edward
B) →
Pawelek, Flora G.
C) →
Pawlowski, Joan M.
D) →
Pawtowski, Wanda
E) →

90. Vanstory, George
A) →
Vanover, Eva
B) →
VanSwinderen, Floyd
C) →
VanSyckle, Harry
D) →
Vanture, Laurence
E) →

GO ON TO THE NEXT COLUMN.

Answers

91. Add:
   2 8
 + 3 5
   ──
A) 53 B) 62
C) 64 D) 73
E) none of these

92. Subtract:
   7 8
 − 6 9
   ──
A) 7 B) 8
C) 18 D) 19
E) none of these

93. Multiply:
   8 6
 ×   6
   ──
A) 492 B) 506
C) 516 D) 526
E) none of these

94. Divide:
   8 / 6 4 8
A) 71 B) 76
C) 81 D) 89
E) none of these

95. Add:
   9 7
 + 3 4
   ──
A) 131 B) 132
C) 140 D) 141
E) none of these

For each question below, find which one of the suggested answers appears in that question.

96. V 5 7 Z N 9 4 T

97. 4 6 P T 2 N K 9

98. 6 4 N 2 P 8 Z K

99. 7 P 5 2 4 N K T

100. K T 8 5 4 N 2 P

Suggested Answers
A = 2, 5, N, Z
B = 4, 5, N, P
C = 2, 9, P, T
D = 4, 9, T, Z
E = none of these

GO ON TO THE NEXT PAGE.

In questions 101 through 105, compare the three names or numbers, and mark the answer

A if ALL THREE names or numbers are exactly ALIKE
B if only the FIRST and SECOND names or numbers are exactly ALIKE
C if only the FIRST and THIRD names or numbers are exactly ALIKE
D if only the SECOND and THIRD names or numbers are exactly ALIKE
E if ALL THREE names or numbers are DIFFERENT

101.	1592514	1592574	1592574
102.	2010202	2010202	2010220
103.	6177396	6177936	6177396
104.	Drusilla S. Ridgeley	Drusilla S. Ridgeley	Drusilla S. Ridgeley
105.	Andrei I. Toumantzev	Andrei I. Tourmantzev	Andrei I. Toumantzov

In questions 106 through 110, find the correct place for the name in the box.

106. Fitzsimmons, Hugh
A) →
  Fitts, Harold
B) →
  Fitzgerald, June
C) →
  FitzGibbon, Junius
D) →
  FitzSimons, Martin
E) →

107. D'Amato, Vincent
A) →
  Daly, Steven
B) →
  D'Amboise, S. Vincent
C) →
  Daniel, Vail
D) →
  DeAlba, Valentina
E) →

108. Schaeffer, Roger D.
A) →
  Schaffert, Evelyn M.
B) →
  Schaffner, Margaret M.
C) →
  Schafhirt, Milton G.
D) →
  Shafer, Richard E.
E) →

109. White-Lewis, Cecil
A) →
  Whitelaw, Cordelia
B) →
  White-Leigh, Nancy
C) →
  Whitely, Rodney
D) →
  Whitlock, Warren
E) →

110. VanDerHeggen, Don
A) →
  VanDemark, Doris
B) →
  Vandenberg, H. E.
C) →
  VanDercook, Marie
D) →
  vanderLinden, Robert
E) →

GO ON TO THE NEXT COLUMN.

Answers

111. Add:
  7 5
  + 4 9
  ———
A) 124   B) 125
C) 134   D) 225
E) none of these

112. Subtract:
  6 9
  − 4 5
  ———
A) 14   B) 23
C) 24   D) 26
E) none of these

113. Multiply:
  3 6
  ×   8
  ———
A) 246   B) 262
C) 288   D) 368
E) none of these

114. Divide:
  8 / 3 2 8
A) 31   B) 41
C) 42   D) 48
E) none of these

115. Multiply:
  5 8
  ×   9
  ———
A) 472   B) 513
C) 521   D) 522
E) none of these

For each question below, find which one of the suggested answers appears in that question.

116. Z 3 N P G 5 4 2

117. 6 N 2 8 G 4 P T

118. 6 N 4 T V G 8 2

119. T 3 P 4 N 8 G 2

120. 6 7 K G N 2 L 5

Suggested Answers
A = 2, 3, G, N
B = 2, 6, N, T
C = 3, 4, G, K
D = 4, 6, K, T
E = none of these

KEY (CORRECT ANSWERS)

1. B	21. A	41. A	61. C	81. D	101. D
2. E	22. E	42. A	62. B	82. C	102. B
3. D	23. E	43. B	63. E	83. A	103. C
4. A	24. D	44. E	64. E	84. D	104. A
5. E	25. C	45. A	65. C	85. B	105. E
6. E	26. D	46. C	66. A	86. A	106. D
7. A	27. D	47. A	67. D	87. E	107. B
8. D	28. C	48. D	68. C	88. C	108. A
9. B	29. C	49. B	69. D	89. C	109. C
10. E	30. D	50. C	70. E	90. B	110. D
11. D	31. E	51. B	71. A	91. E	111. A
12. B	32. A	52. C	72. C	92. E	112. C
13. B	33. A	53. D	73. B	93. C	113. C
14. B	34. C	54. D	74. C	94. C	114. B
15. B	35. C	55. E	75. A	95. A	115. D
16. A	36. E	56. E	76. D	96. D	116. A
17. D	37. A	57. B	77. D	97. C	117. B
18. E	38. C	58. E	78. A	98. E	118. B
19. B	39. C	59. D	79. E	99. B	119. A
20. A	40. D	60. C	80. C	100. B	120. E

ARITHMETICAL REASONING
EXAMINATION SECTION
TEST 1

DIRECTIONS: Each question or incomplete statement is followed by several suggested answers or completions. Select the one that BEST answers the question or completes the statement. *PRINT THE LETTER OF THE CORRECT ANSWER IN THE SPACE AT THE RIGHT.*

1. On March 1, the revenue division of a city department counted $800,000. The money counted on March 2 was 10 percent less than the money counted on March 1.
   If the money counted on March 3 was 10 percent greater than the money counted on March 2, then the money counted on March 3 was

   A. $802,000   B. $792,000   C. $720,000   D. $700,000   1.____

2. If one cashier can count a certain sum of money in 2 hours, and another cashier can count the same sum in 3 hours, then both cashiers working together can count this sum in   2.____

   A. 50 minutes   B. 1 hour 10 minutes
   C. 1 hour 12 minutes   D. 1 hour 20 minutes

3. If the real estate tax is $4.11 per $100 of assessed valuation, the tax on real estate assessed at $195,000 is MOST NEARLY   3.____

   A. $470   B. $6500   C. $8000   D. $9000

4. The tax collections in a tax office for the week ending January 11th were $468,693.80. If this amount was 20 percent greater than the tax collections for the week ending January 4th, the tax collections for the week ending January 4th were MOST NEARLY   4.____

   A. $328,090   B. $375,000   C. $390,580   D. $393,705

5. Assume that the real estate tax rate is $4.08 per $100 of assessed valuation.
   If the tax on a house is $10,404, then the assessed valuation of the house is   5.____

   A. $255,000   B. $240,000   C. $270,000   D. $285,000

6. Cashier X receives payments from 6 taxpayers every 15 minutes. Cashier Y receives payments from 15 taxpayers every half-hour.
   If Cashier X begins work at 9 A.M. and Cashier Y begins work at 9:30 A.M., the time at which the two cashiers will have received payments from an equal number of taxpayers is   6.____

   A. 11 A.M.   B. 11:30 A. M.   C. 12 Noon   D. 12:30 P.M.

7. The real estate tax on a piece of real property in a certain city is $10,824.
   If the assessed valuation of the property is $264,000, then the tax rate per $100 of assessed valuation is   7.____

   A. less than $4.05   B. between $4.05 and $4.08
   C. between $4.09 and $4.14   D. more than $4.14

8. If $300 is invested at simple interest so as to yield a return of $18 in 9 months, the amount of money that must be invested at the same rate of interest so as to yield a return of $120 in 6 months is

8.____

   A. $3,000   B. $3,300   C. $2,000   D. $2,300

9. If a token cost $1.05 and a passenger wants to get 9 tokens without getting any change, he should give you EXACTLY

9.____

   A. $8.10   B. $9.45   C. $9.75   D. $10.50

10. A passenger gives you a twenty-dollar bill and asks for 12 tokens, which cost $1.40 each. You should give the passenger 12 tokens and _____ in change.

10.____

   A. $1. 40   B. $2.40   C. $3.20   D. $4.60

11. 0.16 3/4 written as a percent is

11.____

   A.   16 3/4%   B.   16.3/4%
   C.   0.016 3/4%   D.   0.0016 3/4%

12. $40 reduced by 3/8 of itself is

12.____

   A. $25   B. $65   C. $15   D. $55

13. $1,296.53 minus $264.87 is

13.____

   A. $1,232.76   B. $1,032.76   C. $1,031.66   D. $1,132.53

14. 12 1/2 minus 6 1/4 is

14.____

   A.   5 3/4   B.   6 1/4   C.   6 1/2   D.   5 1/2

15. A desk is marked $98, 20% 30 days, or $98, 30% 15 days cash. If it is paid for in cash immediately on delivery, the amount paid is

15.____

   A. $66.84   B. $63.70   C. $68.40   D. $68.60

16. Add 1/4, 7/12, 3/8, 1/2, and 5/6.

16.____

   A.   2 1/2   B.   2 13/24   C.   2 3/4   D.   2 15/24

17. A floor is 25 ft. wide by 36 ft. long. To cover this floor with carpet will require _____ square yards.

17.____

   A.   100   B.   300   C.   900   D.   25

18. A salesman gets a commission of 4% on his sales. If he wants his commission to amount to $40, he will have to sell merchandise totaling

18.____

   A. $160   B. $10   C. $1,000   D. $100

19. Add 5 hours, 13 minutes; 3 hours, 49 minutes; and 14 minutes. The sum is _____ hours, _____ minutes.

19.____

   A.   8; 16   B.   9; 16   C.   9; 76   D.   8; 6

20. John Doe borrowed $425,000 for 5 years at 9 1/2%. The annual interest charge was   20.____

    A. $25,750   B. $35,750   C. $40,375   D. $42,950

21. 72 divided by .009 is   21.____

    A. .125   B. 800   C. 8,000   D. 80

22. 345 locks at $415 per hundred will cost most nearly   22.____

    A. $14.32   B. $143.20   C. $1,432   D. $14,320

23. The number which, when decreased by 1/5 of itself equals 132, is   23.____

    A. 165   B. 198   C. 98   D. 88

24. 285 is 5% of   24.____

    A. 1,700   B. 7,350   C. 1,750   D. 5,700

25. A store sold suits for $130 each. The suits cost $100 each. The percentage of increase of selling price over cost is   25.____

    A. 40%   B. 33 1/2%   C. 33 1/3%   D. 30%

KEY (CORRECT ANSWERS)

1.	B	11.	A
2.	C	12.	A
3.	C	13.	C
4.	C	14.	B
5.	A	15.	D
6.	B	16.	B
7.	C	17.	A
8.	A	18.	C
9.	B	19.	B
10.	C	20.	C

21.	C
22.	C
23.	A
24.	D
25.	D

SOLUTIONS TO PROBLEMS

1. On March 3rd, amount = ($800,000)(.90)(1.10) = $792,000

2. Let x = minutes working together. Then, x/120 + x/180 = 1 .
   Solving, x = 72 minutes = 1 hour 12 minutes

3. Tax = ($4.11)(195,000 ÷ 100) = $8,014.50 = $8,000

4. For January 4th, tax collections = $468,693.80 * 1.20 ~ $390,580

5. Assessed valuation = ($100)($10,404 ÷ 4.08) = $255,000

6. Every half-hour, cashier X gets payments from 12 taxpayers while cashier Y gets payments from 15 taxpayers. Let n = number of half-hours that cashier X works until both cashiers receive payments from the same number of taxpayers. Since cashier Y begins one half-hour later than X, 12n = 15(n-1). Solving, n = 5. Add 5 half-hours to 9 AM to get 11:30 AM

7. $10,824 ÷ ($264,000 ÷ $100) = $4.10, which is between $4.09 and $4.14.

8. Let R = annual interest rate. Then, $18 = ($300)(R)(9/12).
   Solving, R = .08. Now, let P = principal invested for 6 months. $120 = (P)(.08)(6/12).
   Solving, P = $3000

9. (9)($1.05) = $9.45

10. $20.00 - (12)($1.40) = $3.20 change

11. .16 3/4 = 16 3/4% (just move decimal point 2 places to the right)

12. $40 - (3/8)($40) = $25

13. $1296.53 - $264.87 = $1031.66

14. 12 1/2 - 6 1/4 = 6 1/4

15. ($98)(1-.30) = $68.60

16. 1/4 + 7/12 +3/8 + 1/2 +5/6 = 6/24 +14/24 + 9/24 + 12/24 + 20/24 = 61/24 = 2 13/24

17. (25 ft.)(36 ft.) = 900 sq.ft. = 100 sq.yds.

18. Sales = $40 ÷ .04 = $1000

19. 5 hrs. 13 min. + 3 hrs. 49 min. + 14 min. = 8 hrs. 76 min. = 9 hrs. 16 min.

20. Annual interest = ($425,000)(.095) = $40,375

21. 72 ÷ .009 = 8000

22. ($415)(345 ÷ 100) = $1431.75 = $1432

23. Let n = number. Then, n - 1/5 n = 132. 4/5 n = 132, so n = 165

24. Let n = number. Then, 285 = .05n. Solving, n = 5700

25. $30 ÷ $100 = 30%

———

TEST 2

DIRECTIONS: DIRECTIONS: Each question or incomplete statement is followed by several suggested answers or completions. Select the one that BEST answers the question or completes the statement. *PRINT THE LETTER OF THE CORRECT ANSWER IN THE SPACE AT THE RIGHT.*

1.   Which number is one more than 4,000?   1._____

    A.   3,099   B.   3,900   C.   4,001   D.   3,999

2.   What does MCCXII mean?   2._____

    A.   712   B.   512   C.   802   D.   1,212

3.   What is fifty-two ten-thousandths written as a decimal?   3._____

    A.   52,010,000   B.   .052
    C.   .0052   D.   .00052

4.   What is .127 expressed as a percent?   4._____

    A.   12.7%   B.   1.27%   C.   12 7/100%   D.   12 1/2%

5.   What is seventy billion forty million sixty in figures?   5._____

    A.   70,400,060,000   B.   70,040,600,000
    C.   70,040,000,060   D.   70,040,000,600

6.   What is the equivalent decimal of the fraction 7/8 ?   6._____

    A.   .875   B.   .675   C.   .575   D.   .785

7.   What is the common fraction equivalent (in its lowest terms) of .58 1/3%?   7._____

    A.   5/12   B.   174/300   C.   175/100   D.   7/12

8.   The Health Department reported that 8 out of 12 children had the measles this spring.   8._____
    What fraction shows what proportion of the children had measles?

    A.   8/20   B.   2/3   C.   1/8   D.   1/12

9.   The State census report showed 10,308,252 people in the State.   9._____
    How should this number be written when rounded to the nearest million?

    A.   11,000,000   B.   10,309,000
    C.   10,308,000   D.   10,000,000

10.   When 3/4% of the people of Seattle have been vaccinated for smallpox, what fraction has   10._____
    been vaccinated?

    A.   3/400   B.   1/75   C.   3/4   D.   4/300

11.   What percent of 33 1/3 is 8 1/3?   11._____

    A.   66 2/3%   B.   4%   C.   25%   D.   10%

12. The grades received on a clerical examination were as follows: one received a grade of 90; three received 85; four, 80; two, 75; six, 70; five, 65; two, 60, one, 55; one, 50; one, 45; one, 40; one, 30; and one, 25.
    What was the AVERAGE grade on the examination to the nearest tenth percent?

    A.   85.0%   B.   77.2%   C.   72.7%   D.   66.4%

12.____

13. A clerk saved .16 2/3 of his salary.
    If his salary was $1,800 a month, how many years and months did he work to save $13,500?
    _____ years _____ months.

    A.   3; 9   B.   3; 6   C.   4; 0   D.   3; 3

13.____

14. Folders, each containing the same number of sheets, are filed alphabetically in a 4-drawer cabinet. The inside length of each drawer is 35 inches, and all 4 drawers are packed full. Filed under A are 43 folders occupying 7 inches.
    How many folders are there in the whole cabinet?

    A.   20   B.   215   C.   860   D.   645

14.____

15. A machine operator is paid at the rate of $8.88 per hour if his hourly average production is 250 written bills. For any day in which his hourly average is below 250, his hourly rate of pay is reduced by one-sixth.
    What would be his pay for a seven-hour day in which he produced 1,715 written bills?

    A. $51.80   B. $54.76   C. $60.68   D. $62.16

15.____

16. A stenographer transcribes her notes at the rate of one line typed in ten seconds.
    At this rate, how long, in minutes and seconds, will it take her to transcribe notes which will require seven pages of typing, 25 lines to the page?
    _____ minutes _____ seconds.

    A.   29; 10   B.   17; 50   C.   40; 10   D.   20; 30

16.____

17. During one week, a personnel agency receives 192 applications on Monday, 213 on Tuesday, 218 on Wednesday, 215 on Thursday, 102 on Friday, and 194 on Saturday. If the agency has seven branch offices, what is the daily average number of applications received in each office for the entire week?

    A.   29   B.   27   C.   189   D.   47

17.____

18. Pencils used in an office may be bought at the price of two for 25 cents or, when bought in large quantities, at the price of $6.90 for six dozen.
    What is the savings per dozen when pencils are bought at the lower rate?

    A. $.35   B. $.50   C. $1.85   D. $3.90

18.____

19. If retirement deductions from salaries are increased from 3 1/2% to 5%, what is the monthly amount of the increase in the deduction from an $18,000 salary?

    A. $15.30   B. $52.50   C. $78.30   D. $22.50

19.____

20. A man invested $75,000 in a new business enterprise. The first year, he lost .16 2/3 of   20.____
    his original investment. The next year, he made a profit of 1/3 of his net worth at the
    beginning *of* that year.
    His net worth at the end of the second year was what part of his original investment?

    A.   6 1/4%   B.   75%   C.   80%   D.   93 3/4%

21. Mr. Smith is reconciling his bank balance on November 15th by the use of the following   21.____
    information:

Balance as per bank statement, Oct. 31st	$15,932.20
Total checks outstanding, Oct. 31st	1,642.29
Total deposits, Nov. 1st to Nov. 15th	715.00
Total checks drawn, Nov. 1st to Nov. 15th	1,329.63

According to the above information, the balance that Mr. Smith's checkbook should
show as of the close of business on November 15th is MOST NEARLY

    A. $18,290   B. $16,647   C. $13,675   D. $12,960

22. A bag contains 800 coins. Of these, 10 percent are dimes, 30 percent are nickels, and   22.____
    the rest are quarters.
    The amount of money in the bag is

    A.   less than $150   B.   between $150 and $300
    C.   between $301 and $450   D.   more than $450

Questions 23-25.

DIRECTIONS: Questions 23 through 25 are to be answered on the basis of the following information.

    $100 in pennies weighs 68 pounds, $50 in nickels weighs 11 pounds, $1,000 in silver of
any denomination weighs 54 pounds, and 1,000 tokens weigh 3 pounds 14 ounces.

23. The weight of $77 in pennies is MOST NEARLY _____ pounds.   23.____

    A.   52   B.   48   C.   54   D.   60

24. If a token is worth $1.40 and the tokens in a bag weigh one pound 15 ounces, then the   24.____
    value of these tokens is

    A. $200   B. $700   C. $20   D. $340

25. The contents of a bag containing halves, dimes, and quarters weigh 38 pounds.   25.____
    The amount of money in the bag is MOST NEARLY

    A. $234   B. $380   C. $750   D. $704

KEY (CORRECT ANSWERS)

1.	C		11.	C
2.	D		12.	D
3.	C		13.	A
4.	A		14.	C
5.	C		15.	A
6.	A		16.	A
7.	D		17.	B
8.	B		18.	A
9.	D		19.	D
10.	A		20.	D

21. C
22. A
23. A
24. B
25. D

SOLUTIONS TO PROBLEMS

1. 4000 + 1 = 4001

2. MCCXII = 1000 + (2)(100) + 10 + (2)(1) = 1212

3. Fifty-two ten-thousandths = .0052

4. .127 = 12.7% (Just move decimal 2 places to the right)

5. Seventy billion forty million sixty = 70,040,000,060

6. 7/8 = .875

7. .58 1/3% = 58 1/3 / 100 = 175/300 = 7/12

8. 8/12 = 2/3

9. 10,308,252 is rounded off to the nearest million as 10,000,000

10. 3/4%=3/4

11. $8\dfrac{1}{3} \div 33\dfrac{1}{3} = (\dfrac{22}{3})(\dfrac{3}{100}) = \dfrac{25}{100} = 25\%$

12. [90+(3)(85)+(4)(80)+(2)(75)+(6)(70)+(5)(65)+(2)(60)+55+50+45 +40+30+25] ÷ 29 =

    1925 ÷ 29 ≈ 66.4%

13. ($1800)(.16 2/3) = $300 saved each month. Then, $13,500 ÷ $300 = 45 months = 3 years 9 months

14. Total number of folders = (4)(43)(35/7) = 860

15. Since 1715 < (7)(250), his hourly wage = ($8.88)(5/6) = $7.40 Then, ($7.40)(7) = $51.80

16. (25)(7)(10) = 1750 seconds = 29 minutes 10 seconds

17. Average daily number for agency = (192+213+218+215+102+194) / 6 = 189. Since there are 7 branches, average per branch per day = 189 ÷ 7 = 27

18. At higher rate, cost per dozen = (.25)(12/2) = $1.50, whereas at the lower rate, cost per dozen = $6.90 ÷ 6 = $1.15. Savings = .35

19. $18.000 ÷ 12 = $1500. Increase = (1500)(.05) - (1500)(.035) = $22.50

20. Net worth at end of first year : (75,000 - .17 x 7500) = (75,000 - 12750) = 62250 Net worth at end of second year: (62,250 + 1/3 x 20,750) = 83,000, which is

    $(\dfrac{83,000}{75,000} \times 100)\%$ of his original investment. $= \quad = \dfrac{332}{3}\% = 110\dfrac{2}{3}\%$

21. Balance = $15,932.20 + $715.00 - $1642.29 - $1329.63 $\approx$ $13,675

22. There are 80 dimes, 240 nickels, and 480 quarters.
    Total value = (80)(.10) + (240)(.05) + (480)(.25) = $140, which is less than $150

23. $77 in pennies weighs (77)(68/100) 52 pounds

24. If 1000 tokens weigh 62 ounces, then 31 ounces of tokens represent 500 tokens = (500)(1.40) = $700

25. Dollar value = ($1000)(38/54) $\approx$ $704

TEST 3

DIRECTIONS: Each question or incomplete statement is followed by several suggested answers or completions. Select the one that BEST answers the question or completes the statement. *PRINT THE LETTER OF THE CORRECT ANSWER IN THE SPACE AT THE RIGHT.*

1. Assume that the United States Mint produces 1 million nickels a month. The TOTAL value of the nickels produced during a year is   1._____

    A. $6,000   B. $60,000   C. $600,000   D. $6,000,000

2. If 0.35 is multiplied by 3/5, the answer is   2._____

    A. 0.07   B. 0.21   C. 0.7   D. 2.1

3. Add $26,414.40 to $742.30. From this sum, subtract $42.15. The answer is   3._____

    A. $27,114.55   B. $27,113.30
    C. $27,112.40   D. $27,111.90

4. If 37.14 is multiplied by 0.24, the answer is   4._____

    A. 8.9136   B. 12.4256   C. 89.136   D. 124.256

5. If you add 47.25, 93.15, 142.75, and 0.35, the answer is   5._____

    A. 282.50   B. 282.90   C. 283.30   D. 283.50

6. If a dozen bag seals cost 37 cents, then 768 bag seals cost   6._____

    A. $22.48   B. $23.18   C. $23.68   D. $28.42

7. Since 1965, newly-minted dimes have been composed MAINLY of copper and   7._____

    A. nickel   B. silver   C. zinc   D. tin

8. If a cashier adds $117.98 and $57.03, and then multiplies the total by 2, the answer he SHOULD get is   8._____

    A. $275.02   B. $350.02   C. $450.02   D. $550.02

9. Assume that each of six cashiers counts coins at the same rate of speed. If these six cashiers can count 12,000 coins in 4 hours, then this same number of coins can be counted by 4 cashiers in _____ hours.   9._____

    A. 2   B. 4   C. 6   D. 8

10. Half dollars are usually wrapped in packages of 20, quarters in packages of 40, dimes in packages of 50, and nickels in packages of 40.
The TOTAL amount of money in one package of half dollars, one package of quarters, one package of dimes, and one package of nickels is   10._____

    A. $22   B. $25   C. $27   D. $32

11. Subtract 1,474.50 from the sum of 947.20 and 2,632.80. The answer is   11._____

    A. 2,105.50   B. 2,106.20   C. 2,106.80   D. 2,107.40

12. If 44.8 is divided by 0.4, the answer is   12.____

    A. 1.12   B. 11.2   C. 112   D. 1120

13. If each token is worth 35 cents, then 7,493 tokens are worth a total of   13.____

    A. $2,501.45   B. $2,622.55   C. $2,702.05   D. $2,997.20

14. Divide 924.70 by 0.35.   14.____
    The answer is

    A. 2636   B. 2639   C. 2642   D. 2648

15. Five cashiers can count a certain number of coins in 30 hours.   15.____
    Assuming that each cashier works at the same speed, then three of these cashiers
    can count the same number of coins in _____ hours.

    A. 18   B. 36   C. 42   D. 50

16. The value of four million quarters is   16.____

    A. $1,000,000   B. $100,000
    C. $10,000   D. $1,000

Questions 17-25.

DIRECTIONS: In answering Questions 17 through 25, the worth of a token shall be consid-
                  ered to be 35 cents.

17. The MAXIMUM number of tokens a passenger can purchase when he gives you $4.50 is   17.____

    A. 11   B. 12   C. 13   D. 14

18. A passenger who purchased 9 tokens and received $.10 in change MOST likely gave   18.____
    you a total amount of

    A. $2.50   B. $2.75   C. $3.15   D. $3.25

19. The TOTAL amount of money represented by seven $5 bills, seventeen $1 bills, 11 half-   19.____
    dollars, 58 quarters, 89 dimes, and 86 nickels is

    A. $55.20   B. $62.40   C. $83.40   D. $85.20

20. If a passenger wants to obtain 18 tokens without getting any change, he should give you   20.____
    _____ quarters, _____ dimes, and _____ nickels.

    A. 14; 22; 16   B. 17; 10; 8
    C. 15; 16; 19   D. 19; 24; 12

21. Subtract the total of 9 quarters, 17 dimes, and 12 nickels from the total of 6 half-dollars,   21.____
    14 quarters, 8 dimes, and 6 nickels.
    The answer is

    A. $2.05   B. $3.05   C. $3.15   D. $4.15

22. If a passenger who has no coins wants to obtain 15 tokens and he gets 75 cents in   22.____
    change, the PROPER amount that he should give is

    A. $5.00   B. $6.00   C. $7.00   D. $8.00

23. If a passenger wants to obtain 12 tokens without getting any change, he should give you   23.____
_____ quarters, _____ dimes, _____ nickels.

    A.   10; 6; 18   B.   12; 9; 15
    C.   8; 12; 12   D.   0; 38; 8

24. The TOTAL amount of money represented by 23 quarters, 41 dimes, and 17 nickels is   24.____

    A. $9.60   B. $9.80   C. $10.70   D. $10.80

25. A passenger gives you a $5 bill and asks for seven tokens. The clerk should give the pas-   25.____
senger seven tokens and _____ in change.

    A. $2.05   B. $2.45   C. $2.55   D. $2.85

KEY(CORRECT ANSWERS)

1. C		11. A	
2. B		12. C	
3. A		13. B	
4. A		14. C	
5. D		15. D	
6. C		16. A	
7. A		17. B	
8. B		18. D	
9. C		19. D	
10. C		20. C	

21. B
22. B
23. D
24. C
25. C

SOLUTIONS TO PROBLEMS

1. $(12)(1,000,000)(.05) = \$600,000$

2. $(.35)(3/5) = .21$

3. $\$26,414.40 + \$742.30 - \$42.15 = \$27,114.55$

4. $(37.14)(.24) = 8.9136$

5. $47.25 + 93.15 + 142.75 + .35 = 283.50$

6. $(768 \div 12)(.37) = \$23.68$

7. Post-1965 dimes are composed mainly of copper and nickel.

8. $(\$117.98 + \$57.03)(2) = \$350.02$

9. Let x = number of required hours. Then, $(6)(4) = 4x$ Solving, $x = 6$

10. $(20)(.50) + (40)(.25) + (50)(.10) + (40)(.05) = \$27.00$

11. $947.20 + 2632.80 - 1474.50 = 2105.50$

12. $44.8 \div .4 = 112$

13. $(7493)(.35) = \$2622.55$

14. $924.70 \div .35 = 2642$

15. Let x = number of required hours.
    Then, $(5)(30) = 3x$. Solving, $x = 50$

16. $(4,000,000)(.25) = \$1,000,000$

17. $\$4.50 \div .35 = 12.86$, rounded down to 12 tokens

18. $(9)(.35) + .10 = \$3.25$

19. $(7)(\$5.00) + (17)(\$1.00) + (11)(.50) + (58)(.25) + (89)(.10) + (86)(.05) = \$85.20$

20. $(18)(.35) = \$6.30 = 15$ quarters, 16 dimes, and 19 nickels

21. $[(6)(.50) + (14)(.25) + (8)(.10) + (6)(.05)] - [(9)(.25) + (17)(.10) + (12)(.05)] = \$7.60 - \$4.55$
    $= \$3.05$

22. $(15)(.35) + .75 = \$6.00$

23. $(12)(.35) = \$4.20 = 0$ quarters, 38 dimes, and 8 nickels

24. $(23)(.25) + (41)(.10) + (17)(.05) = \$10.70$

25. $\$5.00 - (7)(.35) = \$2.55$

ARITHMETICAL REASONING
EXAMINATION SECTION
TEST 1

DIRECTIONS: Each question or incomplete statement is followed by several suggested answers or completions. Select the one that BEST answers the question or completes the statement. *PRINT THE LETTER OF THE CORRECT ANSWER IN THE SPACE AT THE RIGHT.*

1. At a certain city garage, there are 216 cars. Of these, 1/2 are assigned to Department P, 1/3 to Department Q, 1/9 to Department R, and the rest to Department S. How many cars are assigned to Department S?

    A. 9   B. 12   C. 18   D. 24

1._____

2. In August a car travels 572 miles; in September, 438 miles; in October, 898 miles; and in December it travels 609 miles. If the five month average from August through December was 673 miles traveled a month, then the number of miles traveled in November was

    A. 638   B. 706   C. 774   D. 848

2._____

3. Suppose the Units R, S, and T gave out a total of 1,715 parking tickets. If Unit R gave out twice as many tickets as Unit S, and Unit T gave out twice as many tickets as Unit R, the number of tickets given out by Unit S is

    A. 270   B. 255   C. 245   D. 225

3._____

4. A car travels at the average rate of 40 miles an hour on the highway. If it takes 5 hours to make a trip of 150 miles, 2/3 of which is on the highway and the rest on city streets, what was the AVERAGE rate of speed of the car on city streets?

    A. 20   B. 25   C. 30   D. 35

4._____

5. A motorist uses 27 gallons of gas on a trip of 351 miles. How many gallons of gas would he use if he took a trip of 624 miles under the same condition?

    A. 45   B. 46   C. 47   D. 48

5._____

6. If the taxi rate in the city is 35 for the first 1/5 of a mile and 5 for each additional 1/5 of a mile, how far did a passenger travel whose fare was 95¢?
_____ miles.

    A. 2 1/5   B. 2 3/5   C. 3 2/5   D. 3 4/5

6._____

7. If you drove a car for three-quarters of an hour and kept it at a steady speed of 30 miles per hour for half an hour and a steady speed of 40 miles per hour the rest of the time, you would have traveled _____ miles.

    A. 20   B. 25   C. 30   D. 35

7._____

8. The length of curb available for the parking of cars on a certain street is 435 feet on the south side and 405 feet on the north side.
Assuming that the bumper-to-bumper length of the average car to be parked is 15 feet, the TOTAL number of cars that can be parked bumper-to-bumper on both sides of the street will be

   A. 56   B. 58   C. 60   D. 61

8._____

9. If the charges against a certain vehicle total $2,000 a year, and 7 1/2% of this is for repairs and maintenance, then the annual cost of repairs and maintenance for that vehicle is

   A. $50   B. $100   C. $150   D. $300

9._____

10. A 210 foot by 120 foot parking lot is reduced in size by construction of a 36 foot by 54 foot building at one of its corners.
The area left for parking is MOST NEARLY _____ square yards.

   A. 1,800   B. 2,600   C. 22,800   D. 23,300

10._____

11. A dispatcher works a total of 44 hours, spending 17 on Special Project A, 13 on Special Project B, and the rest on his usual duties.
The percentage of time he spends on the two special projects is MOST NEARLY

   A. 68%   B. 69%   C. 70%   D. 71%

11._____

12. A driver, dispatched from the garage at 8:15 A.M., arrived at his first destination 35 minutes later. He waited 50 minutes at this location before he could go on to his next destination. It took him one hour and 40 minutes traveling time to get to this second location. He then took an hour lunch period before driving back to the garage, a trip that took 45 minutes.
What time did the driver return to the garage?

   A. 12:25 P.M.   B. 12:45 P.M.
   C. 1:05 P.M.   D. 1:25 P.M.

12._____

13. Truck A has been driven 38,742.3 miles, Truck B has been driven 24,169.7 miles, Truck C has been driven 41,286.4 miles, Truck D has been driven 15,053.5 miles, and Truck E has been driven 8,407.0 miles.
The total mileage of these five trucks combined is MOST NEARLY _____ miles.

   A. 127,650   B. 127,660   C. 128,650   D. 128,660

13._____

14. Suppose that the trucks in a certain garage used a total of 86,314 gallons of gas in 1991 and 8,732 gallons less in 1992.
If they used a total of 72,483 gallons of gas in 1993, how much LESS gas was used in 1993 than in 1992?
_____ gallons.

   A. 5,099   B. 5,109   C. 5,199   D. 5,209

14._____

15. A driver averaged 17 miles for each gallon of gas used one week and 26 miles the next week.
If he used 38.9 gallons during the first week and 27.6 during the second, the TOTAL number of miles he drove in these two weeks was

   A. 1,266.3   B. 1,322.6   C. 1,378.9   D. 1,435.2

15._____

16. In Garage A, 87 drivers worked a total of 427 hours overtime. In Garage B, 53 drivers worked a total of 245 hours overtime.
Compared to the average overtime worked per man in Garage B, the average overtime worked per man in Garage A was MOST NEARLY _____ of an hour _____.

    A. 2/10; more   B. 2/10; less
    C. 3/10; more   D. 3/10; less

16.____

17. The scale on a map indicates that every 1 5/8 inches on the map represents 5 miles. If two locations are 13 inches apart on the map, what is the distance between them in miles?

    A. 30   B. 35   C. 40   D. 45

17.____

18. The number of yards in a mile is

    A. 5,280   B. 1,760   C. 880   D. 440

18.____

19. Add the following numbers: 17 1/2, 29 1/2, and 6 1/2. The CORRECT total is

    A. 32   B. 42   C. 53 1/2   D. 96 1/2

19.____

20. Add 1,516 and 3,497; then subtract 766.
The CORRECT answer is

    A. 2,731   B. 4,247   C. 5,357   D. 5,779

20.____

21. Add 39, 24, and 36. Then divide the total by 3.
The CORRECT answer is

    A. 23   B. 33   C. 96   D. 99

21.____

22. A certain paint can cover 310 square feet per gallon. The number of gallons of this paint required to paint 200 lines each 6 inches wide and 18 feet 6 inches long is MOST NEARLY

    A. 2   B. 4   C. 6   D. 8

22.____

23. A white paint that can cover 500 square feet of surface per gallon is used to paint the crosswalks at street intersections.
If the area at each intersection is equal to 300 square feet, the number of gallons required to paint 50 intersections is

    A. 10   B. 20   C. 30   D. 40

23.____

24. The dimension 45" expressed in feet is

    A. 3 1/3   B. 3 1/2   C. 3 3/4   D. 3 7/8

24.____

25. 85 percent of $5,250 is

    A. $3,463.50   B. $4,361.50
    C. $4,462.50   D. $4,666.50

25.____

KEY (CORRECT ANSWERS)

1.	B		11.	A
2.	D		12.	C
3.	C		13.	B
4.	A		14.	A
5.	D		15.	C
6.	B		16.	C
7.	B		17.	C
8.	A		18.	B
9.	C		19.	C
10.	B		20.	B

21.	B
22.	C
23.	C
24.	C
25.	C

————

SOLUTIONS TO PROBLEMS

1. (1 - 1/2 - 1/3 -1/9)(216) = 12 cars

2. Let x = miles traveled in November. Then, (572+438+898+x+609)/5 = 673. Solving, x = 848

3. Let 2x, x, 4x = number of tickets respectively issued by R, S, T. Then, 2x + x + 4x = 1715. Solving, x = 245

4. Let x = speed on city streets. Then, $\frac{100}{40} + \frac{50}{x} = 5$ Simplifying, 100x + 2000 = 200x. Solving, x = 20 mph.

5. 351 ÷ 27 = 13 miles per gallon. Then, 624 ÷ 13 = 48 gallons

6. Let x = number of miles. Then, .35 + .25(x - 1/5)= .95 Solving, x = 2 3/5

7. (30x.50) + (40x.25) = 25 miles

8. (435+405)/15 = 56 cars

9. Annual cost of repairs and maintenance = (.075)($2000) = $150

10. Area left = (210')(120') - (36')(54) = 23,256 sq.ft., closest to 23,300 sq.ft. ≈ 23,300 ÷ 9 ≈ 2600 sq.yds.

11. (13+17)/44 = $68.\overline{18}$% ≈ 68%

12. 8:15 AM + 35 min. + 50 min. + 1 hr. 40 min. + 1 hr. +45 min. = 8:15 AM + 4 hrs. 50 min. = 1:05 PM

13. 38,742.3 + 24,169.7 + 41,286.4 + 15,053.5 + 8407.0 = 127,658.9 ≈ 127,660 miles

14. 86,314 - 8732 - 72,483 = 5099 gallons less

15. (38.9)(17) + (27.6)(26) = 1378.9 miles

16. Garage A: 427/87 ≈ 4.9   Garage B:245/53 ≈ 4.6
So, average overtime was 3/10 of an hour more in Garage A

17. 13 ÷ 1 5/8 = 8. Then, (8X5) = 40 miles

18. 1 mile = 5280 ÷ 3 = 1760 yds.

19. 17 1/2 + 29 1/2 + 6 1/2 = 53 1/2

20. 1516 + 3497 - 766 = 4247

21. (39+24+36) ÷ 3 = 99 ÷ 3 = 33

22. (200)(1/2')(18 1/2') = 1850 sq.ft. Then, 1850 ÷ 310 ≈ 6 gallons

23. (50)(300 sq.ft.) = 15,000 sq.ft. Then, 15,000 ÷ 500 = 30 gallons

24. 45" = 45/12 = 3 3/4 ft.

25. ($5250)(.85) = $4462.50

―――――

TEST 2

DIRECTIONS: Each question or incomplete statement is followed by several suggested answers or completions. Select the one that BEST answers the question or completes the statement. *PRINT THE LETTER OF THE CORRECT ANSWER IN THE SPACE AT THE RIGHT.*

1. A vehicle which averages 14 1/2 miles to a gallon of gas uses a quart of oil for every 2 1/2 gallons of gas.
   If the vehicle traveled 19,952 miles in a year, its oil consumption for the year would be _____ quarts.

   A. 52   B. 56   C. 60   D. 64

1._____

2. Thirteen percent of all the vehicles in a certain garage are trucks.
   If there are 26 trucks, then the number of vehicles of other types in this garage is

   A. 174   B. 200   C. 260   D. 338

2._____

3. Of 12 employees in a garage, four earn $35,000 a year, two earn $31,500 a year, one earns $45,500 a year, and the rest each earn $38,000 a year.
   The average yearly salary of these employees is CLOSEST to

   A. $35,500   B. $36,500   C. $37,500   D. $38,500

3._____

4. A garage bin used for storing supplies and parts measures 1 yard x 2 yards x 7 feet.
   The cubic volume of this bin is

   A. 5 1/3 cubic yards   B. 16 cubic feet
   C. 63 cubic feet   D. 126 cubic feet

4._____

5. A garage has a gas tank with a capacity of 1,300 gallons. If there are only 520 gallons of gas in the tank, then the tank is _____ full.

   A. 40%   B. 33 1/3%   C. 25%   D. 16 3/4%

5._____

6. Of a specially selected group of vehicles, 1/5 are 6 months old, 2/5 are 12 months old, and 2/5 are 15 months old.
   The average age of this group of vehicles is _____ months.

   A. 9   B. 10   C. 11   D. 12

6._____

7. A section of a garage used for parking vehicles measures 162 1/2' x 25 3/4'.
   If each vehicle to be parked in this section requires on the average 84 sq. ft. of parking space, the MAXIMUM number of vehicles that can be parked in this section is CLOSEST to

   A. 50   B. 45   C. 40   D. 35

7._____

8. Each of the 23 vehicles in a garage uses an average of 114 gallons of gas every 4 weeks.
   If the motor vehicle dispatcher is required to re-order gas when the gas tank in the garage shows no more than a one week supply, he MUST re-order when the gas tank shows _____ gallons.

   A. 655   B. 705   C. 830   D. 960

8._____

9. An employee's annual salary is $45,800. His total annual deductions are 22% for with-holding tax, 8% for pension and social security, and $1,820 for health insurance. The take-home pay that this employee would get on the check he receives every other week is MOST NEARLY

    A. $577.10   B. $845.00   C. $1,154.20   D. $1,220.40

9.____

10. The list price of truck A is $12,500 and that of truck B is $12,000.
If the discount on truck A is 20% and the discount on truck B is 10%, how much cheaper would it be to buy truck A instead of truck B?

    A. $800   B. $450   C. $400   D. No cheaper

10.____

11. There are three garages located in a single block. Garage A has 3/4 of the capacity of garage B and 2/3 of the capacity of garage C.
If 88 cars can be parked in garage B, the TOTAL number of cars that can be parked in all of the three garages is

    A. 186   B. 205   C. 238   D. 253

11.____

12. The city purchases 5 vehicles costing $6,000 each, 3 vehicles costing $8,000 each, and 2 vehicles costing $13,000 each.
The TOTAL cost of these vehicles is

    A. $67,000   B. $26,000   C. $80,000   D. $84,000

12.____

13. A car that averages 15 miles per gallon of gas is driven 135 miles. The gas tank is then filled to capacity by pumping in 12 gallons of gas.
If the gas tank holds 18 gallons when full, the amount of gas in the tank at the begin-ning of the 135 mile trip must have been _____ gallons.

    A. 6   B. 9   C. 12   D. 15

13.____

14. Suppose that a car ran a total of 9,888 miles in a four-month period from September through December, inclusive. It used 234 gallons of gas in September, 203 gallons in October, 191 gallons in November, and 196 gallons in December.
The AVERAGE number of miles it traveled per gallon of gasoline was

    A. 10   B. 11   C. 12   D. 12 1/2

14.____

15. A government agency has a policy of replacing 1/3 of its vehicles each year. Of the 20 vehicles the agency is requesting in the budget, 95% are replacements.
If the request is granted, the TOTAL number of vehicles in the agency will be

    A. 19   B. 27   C. 58   D. 61

15.____

16. Car A averaged 21 miles to a gallon of gas. Car B averaged 18 miles to a gallon of gas. Each car used 14 gallons of gas.
How many miles more did car A travel than car B?

    A. 42   B. 39   C. 28   D. 14

16.____

17. A garage has a gas tank with a capacity of 500 gallons. During the week, 210 gallons were used and 340 gallons were delivered at the end of the week to fill the tank. How many gallons of gas were in the tank at the beginning of the week?

    A. 160   B. 210   C. 340   D. 370

17.____

18. The list price of vehicle A is $4,200 and that of vehicle B is $3,800. The city can get a discount of 20% of the list price on vehicle A and 10% of the list price on vehicle B. How much cheaper can the city buy vehicle A than vehicle B? 18.____

   A. $20   B. $60   C. $200   D. $600

19. In a certain bureau, there are 4 employees who each earn $250 a week, 12 employees who each earn $300 a week , and 2 employees who each earn $350 a week. The weekly payroll for all these employees is 19.____

   A. $4,900   B. $5,100   C. $5,300   D. $5,500

20. If the average passenger car needs 120 square feet of parking space, the LARGEST number of such cars that could be parked in a garage with a usable floor area that measures 70 feet by 100 feet is 20.____

   A. 52   B. 54   C. 56   D. 58

21. On a certain bridge, the toll for a motorcycle is 5/7 the toll for a passenger car and 1/3 the toll for a truck. If the toll for a passenger car is $1.75 then the toll for a truck on this bridge is 21.____

   A. $2,50   B. $3.75   C. $5.00   D. $6.25

22. If a car is traveling on a highway at a steady speed of 35 miles an hour, how many miles will it go in a period of 24 minutes? 22.____

   A. 13   B. 14   C. 15   D. 16

23. An employee's monthly salary is $7,625.
   If he receives a 5.4% salary increase, his new monthly salary will be 23.____

   A. $7,992.50   B. $8,036.75   C. $8,147.25   D. $8,169.00

24. Of the 60 drivers assigned to a garage, 1/6 of them live in County A, 1/4 of them live in County B, 1/5 of them live in County C, and the rest live in County D. How many of the drivers live in County D? 24.____

   A. 22   B. 23   C. 24   D. 25

25. Driver Green travels 33 miles along express highways at an average speed of 44 miles an hour to get to his destination. Driver Smith travels 28 miles through traffic at an average speed of 21 miles an hour to get to the same destination. If Mr. Smith starts his trip a half hour before Mr. Green, he will reach the destination _____ Mr. Green. 25.____

   A. 5 minutes before   B. at the same time as
   C. 5 minutes after   D. 10 minutes after

KEY (CORRECT ANSWERS)

1.	D	11.	D
2.	A	12.	C
3.	B	13.	D
4.	D	14.	C
5.	A	15.	C
6.	D	16.	A
7.	A	17.	D
8.	A	18.	B
9.	C	19.	C
10.	A	20.	D

21.	B
22.	B
23.	B
24.	B
25.	C

SOLUTIONS TO PROBLEMS

1. 19,952 ÷ 14 1/2 = 1376 gallons of gas. Then, 1376 ÷ 21 1/2 = 64 quarts of oil

2. 26 ÷ .13 = 200 vehicles, including the trucks. The number of non-trucks = 200 - 26 = 174

3. [(4)($35,000)+(2)($31,500)+(1)($45,500)+(5)($38,000)] ÷ 12 = $36,541.67, closest to $36,500

4. (3 ft)(6 ft)(7 ft) = 126 cu.ft.

5. 520 ÷ 1300 = 40% full

6. [(1)(6)+(2)(12)+(2)(15)] ÷ 5 = 12 mos.

7. (162 1/2)(25 3/4) ÷ 84 ≈ 49.8, closest to 50 vehicles

8. 114 ÷ 44 = 28.5 . Then, (28.5)(23) ≈ 655 gallons

9. $45,800 - (.22)($45,800) - (.085)($45,800) - $1820 = $30,011
   Amount for every other week = $30,011 ÷ 26 ≈ $1154.20

10. ($12,500)(.80) - ($12,000)(.90) = -$800, so truck A is $800 cheaper than truck B.

11. Garage A holds (3/4)(88) =66 cars and garage C holds 66 ÷ 2/3 = 99 cars. Thus, all 3 garages hold 66 + 88 + 99 = 253 cars

12. Total cost = (5)($6000) + (3)($8000) + (2)($13,000) = $80,000

13. Let x = gallons of gas in the tank at the beginning.

    Then, x - 135/15 + 12 = 18. Solving, x = 15

14. Average = 9888 ÷ (234+203+191+196) = 12 miles per gallon

15. (20)(.95) = 19 replacements. Total number of vehicles = (19)(3) + 1 = 58

16. (21)(14) - (18)(14) = 42 miles

17. Let x = number of gallons in the tank at the beginning of the week. Then, x - 210 + 340 = 500. Solving, x = 370

18. ($3800)(.90) - ($4200)(.80) = $60. So, vehicle A is $60 cheaper than vehicle B.

19. (4)($250) + (12)($300) + (2)($350) = $5300

20. (70)(100) ÷ 120 = 58 .$\overline{3}$ so 58 cars is the maximum.

21. (5/7)($1.75) = $1.25 = toll for a motorcycle.Then, the toll for a truck = 1.25 ÷ 1/3 = $ 3.75

22. (35)(24/60) = 14 miles

23. ($7625)(1.054) = $8036.75

24. 60(1 - 1/6 - 1/4 - 1/5) = 23 drivers

25. Green requires 33/44 = 3/4hrs., whereas Smith requires 28/21 = 1 1/3 hr. Since Smith began 1/2 hr. sooner, he will reach his destination 1 1/3 - 1/2 - 3/4 = 1/12 = 5 min. after Green.

TEST 3

DIRECTIONS: Each question or incomplete statement is followed by several suggested answers or completions. Select the one that BEST answers the question or completes the statement. *PRINT THE LETTER OF THE CORRECT ANSWER IN THE SPACE AT THE RIGHT.*

1. Thirty miles per hour is equivalent to _____ feet per second.   1._____

   A.   30   B.   44   C.   60   D.   80

2. A driver whose car is parked for 8 hours in an off-street facility where the rate is 50 cents   2._____
   an hour for the first 5 hours and 75 cents an hour thereafter would pay

   A. $6.00   B. $5.75   C. $4.75   D. $4.00

3. An agent has written out 29 summonses for moving violations, 13 summonses for park-   3._____
   ing violations, and 3 summonses for other violations.
   The TOTAL number of summonses he has written out is

   A.   36   B.   42   C.   43   D.   45

4. A driver complains about being ticketed for parking too near a fire hydrant. He insists that   4._____
   his car is *at least 8 yards from the hydrant.*
   If he is right, how far away from the hydrant is his car, in terms of feet rather than
   yards?

   A.   16   B.   24   C.   30   D.   80

5. At the intersection of an avenue and a cross street, the traffic lights have been set so that   5._____
   traffic on the avenue has a green light for 55 seconds followed by a yellow light for 5 seconds, then traffic on the cross street has a green light for 25 seconds followed by a yellow
   light for 5 seconds.
   How long is a complete cycle of lights at this intersection, that is, how much time must
   pass from the moment the light turns from red to green until the moment the light will
   turn from red to green again?
   _____ seconds.

   A.   60   B.   70   C.   80   D.   90

6. An agent has jotted down the following notes on one day's work: 6._____
       8:00-11:30   On duty at intersection as assigned
       11:30 - 12:00   Off duty - lunch
       12:00-2:00   On duty - attending assigned training session
       2:00-4:00   On duty at intersection - replacement came late
   How many on-duty hours do this agent's notes show for this particular day?

   A.   4   B.   7   C.   7 1/2   D.   8

7. If a traffic jam of 78 vehicles occurs at the intersection you are controlling, and if one car   7._____
   can pass through the intersection every 10 seconds, how long will it take to clear these
   78 vehicles out of the intersection?
   _____ minutes.

   A.   5.2   B.   7.8   C.   13.0   D.   15.7

8. An agent issued the following summonses in one day: 12 summonses at $25 each, 5 summonses at $15 each, and 3 summonses at $10 each.
What is the TOTAL amount of the fines for the summonses he gave out on that day?

   A. $305   B. $315   C. $405   D. $485

8.____

9. If the difference in elevation between two intersections 300 feet apart is 6 feet, the grade along the street is

   A. 2%   B. 2   C. 0.002   D. 6%

9.____

10. If on a highway a car passes a given point every 5 seconds, the number of cars per hour passing the given point on the highway is

    A. 360   B. 480   C. 600   D. 720

10.____

11. The cost of concrete paving for a strip of driveway 50 feet long, 10 feet wide, and 6 inches deep, if concrete in place costs $30 per cubic yard, is, in dollars, MOST NEARLY
(27 cubic feet = 1 cubic yard)

    A. 278   B. 318   C. 329   D. 380

11.____

12. The sketch at the right shows a right triangular island at the intersection of three streets on which is installed traffic signals A and B. Traffic conditions have increased and require that an additional traffic light be installed at point C. Electric power for signal C is to be taken from the junction box located at the base of post A and extended to C, as shown by the broken line.
With the distances given as shown, the length of conduit, in feet, required to extend power from A to C is MOST NEARLY

    A. 44   B. 60   C. 83   D. 75

12.____

13. The volume of traffic at a certain location increased from 1,000 to 1,500 vehicles per hour.
The percentage increase of traffic is MOST NEARLY

    A. 33%   B. 50%   C. 60%   D. 40%

13.____

14. During a certain three-month period, the bureau of enforcement issued 239,788 sum-monses. Of these, 37,900 were issued between the hours of 12 Noon and 1 P.M.; 33,350 were issued between 1 P.M. and 2 P.M.; and 23,334 were issued between 2 P.M. and 3 P.M.
What percentage of the total number of summonses issued during this three-month period was issued between 1 P.M. and 3 P.M.?

    A. 22%   B. 24%   C. 26%   D. 28%

14.____

15. A city has 51,489 parking meters. Thirteen percent of them require repairs.
Therefore, the number of meters requiring repairs is MOST NEARLY

    A. 6,690   B. 6,695   C. 6,700   D. 6,705

15.____

16. The following sums of money were collected from parking meters in an eight-week
    period: $15,298, $14,248, $16,873, $18,137, $18,256, $19,342, $18,437, and $15,432.
    Therefore, the total amount collected from these meters for this eight-week period was
    MOST NEARLY

    16.____

    A. $135,150   B. $135,985   C. $136,025   D. $136,543

17. There were 68,937 meters in operation at the end of December. Exactly one year later,
    there were 102,331 meters in operation.
    Therefore, the increase in the number of meters in operation is MOST NEARLY

    17.____

    A. 34,400   B. 33,900   C. 33,400   D. 32,900

18. In a certain city, there are 24,482 parking meters. Of these meters, 3/8 are in Zone A.
    Therefore, the number of meters in Zone A is MOST NEARLY

    18.____

    A. 3,060   B. 8,160   C. 9,180   D. 12,240

19. It costs $55,525 to service 9,995 parking meters.
    Therefore, the cost of servicing one meter is MOST NEARLY

    19.____

    A. $2.50   B. $3.50   C. $4.50   D. $5.50

20. Of 165 parking meters, 0.14 of the total are out of order.
    Therefore, the number of these parking meters out of order is MOST NEARLY

    20.____

    A. 83   B. 23   C. 8   D. 2.31

21. Suppose that a city block on a parking meter collector's route is 260 feet wide by 780 feet
    long.
    Therefore, the area of this block, in square feet, is MOST NEARLY

    21.____

    A. 1,040   B. 2,080   C. 104,000   D. 203,000

22. The base of a container for coin boxes measures 2 feet by 3 feet. The base of the coin
    boxes measures 2 inches by 3 inches.
    The GREATEST number of coin boxes that will fit into the container in a single layer is

    22.____

    A. 36   B. 72   C. 100   D. 144

23. The total collected from parking meters in city A for a 12-month period was $701,790.
    Therefore, the average collected per month for this 12-month period was MOST
    NEARLY

    23.____

    A. $58,481   B. $58,483   C. $58,485   D. $8,421,480

24. It costs $158.46 each week to maintain the parking meters in a certain city.
    Therefore, to maintain these meters for 372 weeks would cost MOST NEARLY

    24.____

    A. $58,950   B. $58,975   C. $59,000   D. $59,025

25. Two attendants earn $6,240 and $6,220 per annum, respectively, exclusive of a bonus of
    $2,640 per annum.
    If both have a pension deduction of 20%, the difference in the pension deduction of the
    two attendants on a semimonthly basis is

    25.____

    A. $1.50   B. $.50   C. $1.00   D. $.17

KEY (CORRECT ANSWERS)

1.	B		11.	A
2.	C		12.	B
3.	D		13.	B
4.	B		14.	B
5.	D		15.	B
6.	C		16.	C
7.	C		17.	C
8.	C		18.	C
9.	A		19.	D
10.	D		20.	B

21. D
22. D
23. B
24. A
25. D

SOLUTIONS TO PROBLEMS

1. Since 60 mi/hr = 88 ft/sec, 30 mi/hr = 44 ft/sec

2. ($.50)(5) + ($.75)(3) = $4.75

3. 29 + 13 + 3 = 45 summonses

4. (8)(3) = 24 feet

5. One cycle = 55 + 5 + 25 + 5 = 90 seconds

6. 3 1/2 + 2 + 2 = 7 1/2 hrs. on duty

7. (78)(10) = 780 sec. = 13 min.

8. (12)($25) + (5)($15) + (3)($10) = $405

9. $\dfrac{6}{300}$ = .02 = 2% grade

10. 60 ÷ 5 = 12 per min. Then, (12)(60) = 720 cars per hr.

11. ($30)(50)(10)(1/2) ÷ 27 ≈ $278

12. Distance from A to C = $\sqrt{30^2 + 53^2} = \sqrt{3709} \approx 60$ ft.

13. $\dfrac{500}{1000}$ = 50% increase

14. (33,350+23,334) ÷ 239,788 = 56,684 ÷ 239,788 ≈ 24%

15. (51,489)(.13) = 6693.57, closest to 6695

16. $15,298 + $14,248 + $16,873 + $18,137 + $18,256 + $19,342 + $18,437 + $15,432 = $136,023, closest to $136,025

17. 102,331 - 68,937 = 33,394, closest to 33,400

18. (3/8)(24,482) = 9180.75, nearest to 9180

19. $55,525 ÷ 9995 ≈ $5.56, closest to $5.50

20. (.14)(165) = 23.1 ≈ 23

21. (260)(780) = 202,800 sq.ft. ≈ 203,000 sq.ft.

22. [(2')(3')] ÷ [(2/12')(3/12')] = 144 coin boxes maximum

23. $701,790 ÷ 12 = $58,483

24. $158.46)(372) = $58,947.12 ≈ $58,950

25. ($6240-$6220)(.20) = $4 per year. This equates to $4 ÷ 24 ≈ 17 cents per half-month.

READING COMPREHENSION
UNDERSTANDING AND INTERPRETING WRITTEN MATERIAL
EXAMINATION SECTION
TEST 1

DIRECTIONS: Each question or incomplete statement is followed by several suggested answers or completions. Select the one that BEST answers the question or completes the statement. *PRINT THE LETTER OF THE CORRECT ANSWER IN THE SPACE AT THE RIGHT.*

Questions 1-9.

DIRECTIONS: Questions 1 through 9, inclusive, are based on the STATE MOTOR VEHICLE BUREAU'S POINT SYSTEM given below. Read this point carefully before answering these items.

STATE MOTOR VEHICLE BUREAU'S POINT SYSTEM

The newly revised point system was effective April 1. After that date, a driver having offenses resulting in an accumulation of eight points within two years, ten points within three years, or twelve points within four years, is to be summoned for a hearing which may result in the loss of his license. Under the point system, three points are charged for speeding, two points for passing a red light or crossing a double line or failing to stop at a stop sign, one and a half points for inoperative horn or insufficient lights, and one point for improper turn or failure to notify Bureau of change of address. The Commissioner of Motor Vehicles is required to revoke a driver's license if he has three speeding violations in a period of 18 months, or drives while intoxicated or leaves the scene of an accident or makes a false statement in his application for a driver's license. This system is necessary because studies show violations of traffic laws cause four out of five fatal accidents in the state.

1. The traffic offense which calls for license revocation if repeated three times within a period of 1 1/2 years is

   A. passing a red light
   B. passing a stop sign
   C. crossing a double line
   D. speeding

1.____

2. The individual who has the power to revoke a driver's license is the

   A. traffic officer
   B. motor vehicle inspector
   C. Commissioner of Motor Vehicles
   D. Traffic Commissioner

2.____

3. Crossing a double line has a penalty of twice as many points as for

   A. making an improper turn   B. speeding
   C. passing a red light   D. an inoperative horn

3.____

4. Failure of a driver to properly notify the Bureau of Motor Vehicles of a change in his address carries a penalty of _____ point(s).   4._____

   A. 1/2   B. 1   C. 1 1/2   D. 2

5. The point system is specifically designed to penalize the driver who   5._____

   A. is inexperienced
   B. repeatedly violates traffic laws
   C. is overage
   D. ignores parking violations

6. A false statement on a driver's license application calls for a penalty of   6._____

   A. 10 points   B. 8 points
   C. license suspension   D. license revocation

7. Insufficient lights carries a penalty of _____ point(s).   7._____

   A. 1/2   B. 1   C. 1 1/2   D. 2

8. A driver is summoned for a hearing if, within a period of three years, he Accumulates _____ points.   8._____

   A. 6   B. 8   C. 10   D. 12

9. The percentage of fatal accidents caused by traffic violations is   9._____

   A. 80%   B. 70%   C. 60%   D. 50%

Questions 10-11.

DIRECTIONS: Questions 10 and 11 are to be answered ONLY according to the information given in the following paragraph.

The State Vehicle and Traffic law was changed effective October 1, 2005 to provide for all new driving licenses to be issued on a six-month probationary basis. The probationary license will be cancelled if during this six-month period the driver is found guilty of tailgating, speeding, reckless driving, or driving while his ability is impaired by alcohol. The license will also be cancelled if the driver is found guilty of two other moving traffic violations. If a probationary license is cancelled, the driver must wait for sixty days after the date of cancellation before applying for another license; and if the application is approved, the applicant must meet certain additional requirements including a new road test before a new license will be issued.

10. It is MOST reasonable to assume that the main purpose of the change in the law referred to above was to   10._____

    A. find out who is responsible for most traffic accidents
    B. make the road tests more difficult for new drivers to pass
    C. make it harder to get a driver's license
    D. serve as a further check on the competence of new drivers

11. According to the above passage, we may assume that a probationary license will NOT be cancelled if a driver is found guilty of

    A. passing a red light and failing to keep to the right on a road
    B. following another vehicle too closely
    C. overtime parking at a meter on two or more occasions
    D. driving at 60 miles an hour on a road where the speed limit is 50 miles an hour

11.____

Questions 12-13.

DIRECTIONS: Questions 12 and 13 are to be answered SOLELY on the basis of the following paragraph.

If a motor vehicle fails to pass inspection, the owner will be given a rejection notice by the inspection station. Repairs must be made within ten days after this notice is issued. It is not necessary to have the required adjustment or repairs made at the station where the inspection occurred. The vehicle may be taken to any other garage. Re-inspection after repairs may be made at any official inspection station, not necessarily the same station which made the initial inspection. The registration of any motor vehicle for which an inspection sticker has not been obtained as required, or which is not repaired and inspected within ten days after inspection indicates defects, is subject to suspension. A vehicle cannot be used on public highways while its registration is under suspension.

12. According to the above paragraph, the owner of a car which does NOT pass inspection must

    A. have repairs made at the same station which rejected this car
    B. take the car to another station and have it re-inspected
    C. have repairs made anywhere and then have the car re-inspected
    D. not use the car on a public highway until the necessary repairs have been made

12.____

13. According to the above paragraph, the one of the following which may be cause for suspension of the registration of a vehicle is that

    A. an inspection sticker was issued before the rejection notice had been in force for ten days
    B. it was not re-inspected by the station that rejected it originally
    C. it was not re-inspected oither by the station that rejected it originally or by the garage which made the repairs
    D. it has not had defective parts repaired within ten days after inspection

13.____

Questions 14-18.

DIRECTIONS: Questions 14 through 18 are to be answered ONLY on the basis of the following paragraphs.

Under the Vehicular Responsibility Law of a certain state, an insurance carrier who has previously furnished the Division of Roads and Vehicles with evidence of a vehicle registrant's financial responsibility (Form VR-1, VR-1A, VR-2B or VR-11) must, in case of termination of insurance, first notify the insured registrant at least 10 days in advance if the termination is due to failure to pay the insurance premium and at least 20 days if the termination is due to any other reason. The insurance carrier must then notify the Division not later than 30 days following the effective date of actual termination of insurance coverage. The only acceptable proof of such termination is Form VR-4.

Upon receipt of Form VR-4 by the Division, a search will be made for any superseding coverage or a record of voluntary surrender of plates and registration certificate on or prior to the effective date of termination. If such a record is found, no further action is taken by the Division. If the Division finds no record of acceptable superseding coverage or timely surrender of plates and registration, Form letter VR-7T is sent to the registrant with a photostatic copy of Form VR-4, providing him with an opportunity to invalidate the proceeding to cancel his registration by submitting additional evidence, which may take the form of proof of continuous financial responsibility, timely sale of the vehicle, or evidence of voluntary surrender of plates and registration certificate. Only after the registrant has failed to comply by one of the above three methods is an order to cancel registration (Form VR-8) issued.

Upon the issuance of a cancellation order, a copy of the order is mailed to the registrant directing him to immediately surrender his plates and registration certificate to a specified area office of the Division. At the same time, two copies of the cancellation order are sent to the area office, where they are held for 15 days. If the registrant complies with the order, he is issued a notice of compliance (Form VR-3). If he fails to comply within the 15 days, two more copies of the order are mailed to the Highway Patrol for enforcement of the cancellation order. No further action is taken for a period of 30 days. If no record of enforcement is received, another copy of the cancellation order is sent to the Police Department as a follow-up.

14. When the Division of Roads and Vehicles receives acceptable evidence that the insurance coverage on a particular registrant has been terminated, it is required FIRST to   14.____

    A. cancel the registration if the insurance was terminated because of failure to pay the insurance premium
    B. notify the registrant to voluntarily surrender his plates and registration certificate on or prior to a certain date
    C. determine whether the registrant has obtained other insurance for that vehicle
    D. send the registrant Form letter VR-7T stating that he must submit evidence to prevent cancellation of his registration

15. In order to comply with the above procedure, the MINIMUM number of copies of the cancellation order that must be prepared, including one to be kept in the central Division of Roads and Vehicles file, is   15.____

    A. 3   B. 4   C. 5   D. 6

16. The one of the following which is required before steps   16.____

    A. the insurance carrier to notify the Division of Roads and Vehicles in writing (VR-11) that the insured registrant's premium payment is 30 days overdue
    B. the registrant to notify the Division of Roads and Vehicles that he either intends to sell or has sold his vehicle
    C. Form VR-8 to be sent to the insured registrant by the Division of Roads and Vehicles
    D. Form VR-4 to be sent by the insurance carrier to the Division of Roads and Vehicles

17. The MAXIMUM amount of time a vehicle registrant is allowed in which to comply with a cancellation order before the police are asked to enforce the order is _____ days.

    A. 30   B. 35   C. 40   D. 45

17.____

18. It would be MOST accurate to state with regard to the issuance of a certificate of compliance that the

    A. Division of Roads and Vehicles issues one to the registrant after he has submitted the additional evidence in response to Form letter VR-7T
    B. Division of Roads and Vehicles may issue one to the registrant at any time after he has been mailed a copy of the cancellation order and before the Highway Patrol is notified
    C. Highway Patrol may issue one to the registrant if he surrenders his plates and registration to them during the 30 days following their receipt of the request for enforcement
    D. Highway Patrol may issue one to the registrant at any time before the Police Department is notified

18.____

Questions 19-22.

DIRECTIONS: Questions 19 through 22 are to be answered ONLY on the basis of the information given in the following paragraph.

All automotive accidents, no matter how slight, are to be reported to the Safety Division by the employee involved on Accident Report Form S-23 in duplicate. When the accident is of such a nature that it requires the filling out of the State Motor Vehicle Report Form MV-104, this form is also prepared by the employee in duplicate and sent to the Safety Division for comparison with the Form S-23. The Safety Division forwards both copies of Form MV-104 to the Corporation Counsel, who sends one copy to the State Bureau of Motor Vehicles. When the information on the Form S-23 indicates that the employee may be at fault, an investigation is made by the Safety Division. If this investigation shows that the employee was at fault, the employee's dispatcher is asked to file a complaint on Form D-11. The foreman of mechanics prepares a damage report on Form D-8 and an estimate of the cost of repairs on Form D-9. The dispatcher's complaint, the damage report, the repair estimate, and the employee's previous accident record are sent to the Safety Division where they are studied together with the accident report. The Safety Division then recommends whether or not disciplinary action should be taken against the employee.

19. According to the above paragraph, the Safety Division should be notified whenever an automotive accident has occurred by means of Form(s)

    A. S-23
    B. S-23 and MV-104
    C. S-23, MV-104, D-8, D-9, and D-11
    D. S-23, MV-104, D-8, D-9, D-11, and employee's accident report

19.____

20. According to the above paragraph, the forwarding of the Form MV-104 to the State Bureau of Motor Vehicles is done by the

    A. Corporation Counsel   B. dispatcher
    C. employee involved in the accident   D. Safety Division

20.____

21. According to the above paragraph, the Safety Division investigates an automotive acci- 21.____
dent if the

    A. accident is serious enough to be reported to the State Bureau of Motor Vehicles
    B. dispatcher files a complaint
    C. employee appears to have been at fault
    D. employee's previous accident report is poor

22. Of the forms mentioned in the above paragraph, the dispatcher is responsible for prepar- 22.____
ing the

    A. accident report form
    B. complaint form
    C. damage report
    D. estimate of cost of repairs

Questions 23-25.

DIRECTIONS: Questions 23 through 25 are to be answered ONLY on the basis of the information given in the following paragraph.

    One of the major problems in the control of city motor equipment, and especially passen-
ger equipment, is keeping the equipment working for the city and for the city alone for as
many hours of the day as is practical. Even when most city employees try to get the most out
of the cars, a poor system of control will result in wasted car hours. Some city employees
have a legitimate use for a car all day long while others use a car only a small part of the day
and then let it stand. As a rule, trucks are easier to control than passenger cars because they
are usually assigned to a specific job where a foreman continually oversees them. Even
though trucks are usually fully utilized, there are times when the normal work assignment
cannot be carried out because of weather conditions or seasonal changes. At such times, a
control system could plan to make the trucks available for other uses.

23. According to the above paragraph, a problem connected with controlling the use of city 23.____
motor equipment is

    A. increasing the life span of the equipment
    B. keeping the equipment working all hours of the day
    C. preventing the overuse of the equipment to avoid breakdowns
    D. preventing the private use of the equipment

24. According to the above paragraph, a good control system for passenger equipment will 24.____
MOST likely lead to

    A. better employees being assigned to operate the cars
    B. fewer city employees using city cars
    C. fewer wasted car hours for city cars
    D. insuring that city cars are used for legitimate purposes

25. According to the above paragraph, a control system for trucks is useful because

    25.____

    A. a foreman usually supervises each job
    B. special conditions sometimes prevent the planned use of a truck
    C. trucks are easier to control than passenger cars
    D. trucks are usually assigned to specific jobs where they cannot be fully utilized

Question 26.

DIRECTIONS: Question 26 is to be answered SOLELY on the basis of the following paragraph.

    Whereas automobile travel in general corresponds to the general motor vehicles index, as represented by total gas usage, traffic trends on one particular road may vary from average. Comparison of the records of various main arteries indicates that automobile travel on some highways has gone up much faster than the general trend of gas usage. The conclusion is that the bulk of local travel remains stable, but a very large share of the total increase in travel is concentrated on main highways. This would be especially true on new highways which provide better means of travel and foster trips which would not have been made if the new route had not been constructed.

26. According to the above paragraph, which one of the following is *most likely* to result in increased automobile travel?

    26.____

    A. A new roadway   B. Stable local conditions
    C. A choice of routes   D. Traffic trends

Questions 27-30.

DIRECTIONS: Questions 27 through 30 are to be answered ONLY on the basis of the following paragraph.

    Analysis of current data reveals that motor vehicle transportation actually requires less space than was used for other types of transportation in the pre-automobile era, even including the substantial area taken by freeways. The reason is that when the fast-moving through traffic is put on built-for-the-purpose arterial roads, then the amount of ordinary space needed for strictly local movement and for access to property drops sharply. Even the amount of land taken for urban expressways turns out to be surprisingly small in terms either of total urban acreage or of the volume of traffic they carry. No existing or contemplated urban expressway system requires as much as 3 percent of the land in the areas it serves, and this would be exceptionally high. The Los Angeles freeway system, when complete, will occupy only 2 percent of the available land; the same is true of the District of Columbia, where only 0.75 percent will be pavement, with the remaining 1.25 percent as open space. California studies estimate that, in a typical California urban community, 1.6 to 2 percent of the area should be devoted to freeways, which will handle 50 to 60 percent of all traffic needs, and about ten times as much land to the ordinary roads and streets that carry the rest of the traffic. By comparison, when John A. Sutter laid out Sacramento in 1850, he provided 38 percent of the area for street and sidewalks. The French architect, Pierre L'Enfant, proposed 59 percent of the area of the District of Columbia for roads and streets; urban renewal in Southwest Washington, incorporating a modern street network, reduced the acreage of space for pedestrian and vehicular traffic in the renewal area from 48.2 to 41.5 percent of the total. If we are to have a reasonable consideration of the impact of highway transportation on contemporary urban development, it would be well to understand these relationships.

27. The author of this passage says that   27.____

    A. modern transportation uses less space than was used for transportation before the auto age
    B. expressways require more space than streets in terms of urban acreage
    C. typical urban communities were poorly designed in terms of relationship between space used for traffic and that used for other purposes
    D. the need for local and access roads would increase if the number of expressways were increased

28. According to the above passage, it was originally planned that the percent of the area to   28.____
be used for roads and streets in the District of Columbia should be MOST NEARLY

    A. 40%   B. 45%   C. 50%   D. 60%

29. The above passage states that the amount of space needed for local traffic   29.____

    A. *increases* when arterial highways are constructed
    B. *decreases* when arterial highways are constructed
    C. *decreases* when there is more land available
    D. *increases* when there is more land available

30. According to the above passage, studies estimate that, land devoted to in a typical Cali-   30.____
fornia urban community, the amount of ordinary roads and streets as compared with that devoted to freeways should be MOST NEARLY as much.

    A. one-half   B. one-tenth
    C. twice   D. ten times

———————

KEY (CORRECT ANSWERS)

1.	D		16.	D
2.	C		17.	D
3.	A		18.	B
4.	B		19.	A
5.	B		20.	A
6.	D		21.	C
7.	C		22.	B
8.	C		23.	D
9.	A		24.	C
10.	D		25.	B
11.	C		26.	A
12.	C		27.	A
13.	D		28.	D
14.	C		29.	B
15.	B		30.	D

TEST 2

DIRECTIONS: Each question or incomplete statement is followed by several suggested answers or completions. Select the one that BEST answers the question or completes the statement. *PRINT THE LETTER OF THE CORRECT ANSWER IN THE SPACE AT THE RIGHT.*

Questions 1-5.

DIRECTIONS: Questions 1 through 5 are to be answered ONLY on the basis of information given in the following passage.

Fatigue can make a driver incompetent. He may become less vigilant. He may lose judgment as to the speed and distance of other cars. His reaction time is likely to be slowed down, and he is less able to resist glare. With increasing fatigue, driving efficiency falls. Finally, nodding at the wheel results, from which accidents follow almost invariably.

Accidents that occur with the driver asleep at the wheel are generally very serious. With the driver unconscious, no effort is made either to prevent the accident or to lessen its seriousness. Accidents increase as day wears on and reach their peak in the early evening and during the first half of the night. Driver fatigue undoubtedly plays a significant part in causing these frequent night accidents.

1. Among the results of fatigue, the passage does NOT indicate   1.____

    A. lessened hearing effectiveness
    B. lessened vigilance
    C. loss of driving efficiency
    D. increased reaction time

2. According to the passage, accidents almost always follow as a result of   2.____

    A. fatigue
    B. slowed down reaction time
    C. nodding at the wheel
    D. lessened vigilance

3. According to the passage, accidents that occur in the early evening and during the first   3.____
   half of the night are

    A. always caused by driver fatigue
    B. very frequently the result of lessened resistance to glare
    C. usually due to falling asleep at the wheel
    D. more frequent than accidents in the afternoon

4. According to the passage, very serious accidents result from   4.____

    A. falling asleep at the wheel
    B. poor driving
    C. lack of judgment
    D. poor vision

5. Referring to the passage, which of the following conclusions is NOT correct?   5.____

    A.   There are only two paragraphs in the entire passage.
    B.   One paragraph contains four sentences.
    C.   There are six words in the first sentence.
    D.   There is no sentence of less than six words.

Questions 6-8.

DIRECTIONS: Questions 6 through 8 are to be answered ONLY according to the information given in the following passage.

Drivers and pedestrians face additional traffic hazards during the fall months. Changing autumn weather conditions, longer hours of darkness, and the abrupt nightfall during the evening rush hour can mean more traffic deaths and injuries unless drivers and pedestrians exercise greater care and alertness. Drivers must adjust to changing light conditions; they cannot use the same driving habits and attitudes at dusk as they do during daylight. Moderate speed and continual alertness are imperative for safe city driving at this time of year.

6. According to the above passage, two new traffic risks which motorists face in the fall are   6.____

    A.   changing weather conditions and more traffic during the evening rush hour
    B.   fewer hours of daylight and sudden nightfall
    C.   less care by pedestrians and a change in autumn weather conditions
    D.   more pedestrians on the street and longer hours of darkness

7. According to the above passage, there may be more traffic deaths and injuries in the fall   7.____
MAINLY because both pedestrians and drivers are

    A.   distracted by car lights being turned on earlier
    B.   hurrying to get home from work in the evening
    C.   confronted with more traffic dangers
    D.   using the streets in greater numbers

8. According to the above passage, an ESSENTIAL requirement of driving safely in the city   8.____
in the fall is

    A.   eyes down on the road at all times
    B.   very slow speed
    C.   no passing
    D.   reasonable speed

Questions 9-11.

DIRECTIONS: Questions 9 through 11 are to be answered ONLY according to the information given in the following passage.

A traffic sign is a device mounted on a fixed or portable support through which a specific message is conveyed by means of words or symbols. It is erected by legal authority for the purpose of regulating, warning, or guiding traffic.

A regulatory sign is used to indicate the required method of traffic movement or the permitted use of a highway. It gives notice of traffic regulations that apply only at specific places or at specific times that would not otherwise be apparent.

A warning sign is used to call attention to conditions on or near a road that are actually or potentially hazardous to the safe movement of traffic.

A guide sign is used to direct traffic along a route or toward a destination, or to give directions, distances or information concerning places or points of interest.

9. According to the above passage, which one of the following is NOT a *regulatory* sign? 9.___

    A. Right turn on red signal permitted
    B. Trucks use right lane
    C. Slippery when wet
    D. Speed limit 60

10. According to the above passage, which one of the following LEAST fits the description of a *warning* sign? 10.___

    A. No right turn
    B. Falling rock zone
    C. Low clearance, 12 ft. 6 in.
    D. Merging traffic

11. According to the above passage, which one of the following messages is LEAST likely to be conveyed by a *guide* sign? 11.___

    A. South bound   B. Signal ahead
    C. Bridge next exit   D. Entering city

Questions 12-14.

DIRECTIONS: Questions 12 through 14 are to be answered ONLY on the basis of the information given in the following passage.

A National Safety Council study of 685,000 traffic accidents reveals that most accidents happen under *safe* conditions—in clear, dry weather, on straight roads, and when traffic volumes are low. The point is most accidents can be attributed to lapses on the part of the drivers rather than traffic or road conditions or deliberate law violations. Most drivers try to avoid accidents. Why, then, do so many get into trouble? A major cause is the average motorist's failure to recognize a hazard soon enough to avoid it entirely. He does not, by habit, notice the clues that are there for him to see. He takes constant risks in traffic without even knowing it. These faulty seeing habits plus the common distractions that all drivers must deal with, such as hurry, worry, daydreaming, impatience, concentration on route problems, add up to a guaranteed answer—an accident.

12. According to a study by the National Safety Council, MOST accidents can be blamed on 12.___

    A. curving, hilly roads   B. errors made by drivers
    C. heavy streams of traffic   D. wet, foggy weather

13. According to the above passage, an IMPORTANT reason why the average motorist gets into an accident is that he 13._____

    A. does not see the danger of an accident soon enough
    B. does not try to avoid accidents
    C. drives at too great a speed
    D. purposely takes reckless chances

14. According to the above passage, it is NOT reasonable to say that drivers are distracted from their driving and possibly involved in an accident because they 14._____

    A. are impatient about something
    B. concentrate on the road ahead
    C. hurry to get to where they are going
    D. worry about some problem

Questions 15-18.

DIRECTIONS: Questions 15 through 18 are to be answered ONLY on the basis of the information given in the following passage.

If a good automobile road map is studied thoroughly before a trip is started, much useful information can be learned. This information may help to decrease the cost of and the time required for the trip and, at the same time, increase the safety and comfort of the trip. The legend found on the face of the map explains symbols and markings and the kind of roads on various routes. The legend also explains how to tell by width, color, or type of line whether the road is dual- or multiple-lane, and whether it is paved, all-weather, graded, earth, under construction, or proposed for construction. Federal routes are usually shown by a number within a shield, and state routes by a number within a circle. The legend also shows scale of miles on a bar marked to indicate the distance each portion of the bar represents on the earth's surface. Distances between locations on the map are shown by plain numerals beside the route lines; they indicate mileage between marked points or intersections. Add the mileage numbers shown along a route to determine distances.

15. According to the above passage, the markings on the road map will show 15._____

    A. a different color for a road proposed for construction than for one under construction
    B. a double line if a road is a dual-lane road
    C. what part of a road is damaged or being repaired
    D. which roads on state routes have more than two lanes

16. The above paragraph does NOT mention as a possible advantage of studying a good road map before beginning a trip the 16._____

    A. increase in interest of the trip
    B. reduction in the chance of an accident on the trip
    C. saving of money
    D. saving of time

17. According to the above passage, in order to find the total mileage of a certain route, a motorist should add the numbers   17._____

    A. on the bar scale in the legend
    B. between marked points beside the route lines
    C. inside a shield along the route
    D. within a circle along the route

18. According to the above passage, the legend on a road map includes information which a motorist could use to   18._____

    A. choose the best paved route
    B. figure the toll charges
    C. find the allowable speed limits
    D. learn the location of bridges

Questions 19-30.

DIRECTIONS: The following is an accident report similar to those used by departments for reporting accidents. Questions 19 through 30 are to be answered ONLY on the basis of the information contained in this accident report.

ACCIDENT REPORT

Date of Accident: April 12, _____   Date of Report: April 15, _____
Place of Accident: 17th Ave. & 22nd St.   Friday
Time of Accident: 10:15 A.M.
City Vehicle: Vehicle No. 2:
Operator's Name: John Smith   Operator's Name: James Jones
Title: Motor Vehicle Operator   Operator's Address: 427 E 198th St.
Badge No.: 17-5427   Operator License No.: J0837-0882-
Operator License No.: S2874-7513-   7851
  3984   Owner's Name: Michael Greene
Vehicle Code No.: B7-8213   Owner's Address: 582 E 92nd St.
License Plate No.: BK-4782   License Plate No.: 6Y-3916
Damage to Vehicle: Left front   Damge to Vehicle: Left front
  fender dented; broken left   bumper bent inward; broken
  front headlight and parking   left front headlight; grille
  light; windshield wipers not   broken in three places
  operating

DESCRIPTION OF ACCIDENT: I was driving on 17th Avenue, a southbound one-way street and made a slow, wide turn west into 22nd Street, a two-way street, because a moving van was parked near the corner on 22nd Street. As I completed my turn, a station wagon going east on 22nd Street hit me. The driver of the station wagon said he put on his brakes but he skidded on some oil that was on the street. The driver of the van saw the accident from his cab and told me that the station wagon skidded as he put on his brakes. Patrolman Jack Reed, Badge #24578, who was at the southeast corner of the intersection, saw what happened and made some notes in his memo book.

Persons Injured - Names and Addresses. If none, state NONE:

Witnesses - Names and Addresses. If none, state NONE:
  Jack Reed, 33-47 83rd Drive
  Thomas Quinn, 527 Flatlands Avenue

Report prepared by: John Smith
Title: Motor Vehicle Operator

19. According to the report, the accident happened on   19.____

  A. Friday, between 6:00 A.M. and 12:00 Noon
  B. Friday, between 12:00 Noon and 6:00 P.M.
  C. Tuesday, between 6:00 A.M. and 12:00 Noon
  D. Monday, between 12:00 Noon and 6:00 P.M.

20. Which one of the following numbers is part of the driver's license of the operator of the   20.____
    city vehicle?

  A. 3984   B. 5247   C. 4782   D. 7851

21. The address of the driver of the city vehicle is   21.____

  A. not given in the report   B. 427 E 198th Street
  C. 582 E 92nd Street   D. 33-47 83rd Drive

22. A section of the report that is NOT properly filled out is   22.____

  A. Witnesses   B. Description of Accident
  C. Persons Injured   D. Damage to Vehicle

23. According to the accident report, if the only witnesses were the patrolman and the van   23.____
    driver, then the van driver's name is

  A. Reed   B. Quinn   C. Jones   D. Greene

24. According to the report, the diagram that would BEST show where the cars collided and   24.____
    where the moving van (|v|) was parked at the time of the accident is

25. According to the information in the report, it would be MOST correct to say that Michael   25.____
Greene was

    A. the driver of the station wagon
    B. a passenger in the station wagon
    C. the owner of the moving van
    D. the owner of the station wagon

26. According to the information in the report, a factor which contributed to the accident was   26.____

    A. a slippery road condition
    B. bad brakes of one car
    C. obstructed view of traffic light caused by parked van
    D. windshield wipers on the city car not operating properly

27. When a driver makes a report such as this, it is MOST important that he   27.____

    A. print the information so that his supervisor can read it quickly
    B. keep it short because a long report makes it look as though he is hiding a mistake behind many words
    C. show clearly why the accident isn't his fault
    D. give all the facts accurately and completely

28. The first two letters or numbers in the City Vehicle Code Number indicate the type of   28.____
vehicle. Two letters indicate an 8 passenger 8-cylinder car; two numbers indicates a 6
passenger 8-cylinder car; a letter followed by a number indicates a 6 passenger 6-cylin-
der car; a number followed by a letter indicate an 8-cylinder station wagon.
The city car involved in this accident is, therefore, a(n)

    A. 8-cylinder station wagon
    B. 6 passenger 6-cylinder car
    C. 6 passenger 8-cylinder car
    D. 8 passenger 8-cylinder car

29. From the information in the report, the driver of the city vehicle may have been partially at   29.____
fault because he

    A. appears to have begun his turn from the wrong lane
    B. appears to have entered the wrong lane of traffic
    C. did not blow his horn as he made the turn
    D. should have braked as he made the turn

30. What evidence is there in the report that the two vehicles collided in front, driver's side?   30.____

    A. The description of the accident
    B. There is no such evidence
    C. The type of damage to the vehicles
    D. The van driver's statement

KEY (CORRECT ANSWERS)

1.	A		16.	A
2.	C		17.	B
3.	D		18.	A
4.	A		19.	C
5.	D		20.	A
6.	B		21.	A
7.	C		22.	C
8.	D		23.	B
9.	C		24.	D
10.	A		25.	D
11.	B		26.	A
12.	B		27.	D
13.	A		28.	B
14.	B		29.	B
15.	D		30.	C

TEST 3

DIRECTIONS: Each question or incomplete statement is followed by several suggested answers or completions. Select the one that BEST answers the question or completes the statement. *PRINT THE LETTER OF THE CORRECT ANSWER IN THE SPACE AT THE RIGHT.*

Questions 1-7.

DIRECTIONS: Questions 1 through 7, inclusive, are based on the paragraph below. Refer to this paragraph in answering these questions.

DRINKING AND DRIVING

In fatal traffic accidents, a drinking driver is involved more than 30% of the time; on holiday weekends, more than 50% of the fatal accidents involve drinking drivers. Drinking to any extent reduces the judgment, self-control, and driving ability of any driver. Social drinkers, especially those who think they drive better after a drink, are a greater menace than commonly believed, and they outnumber the obviously intoxicated. Two cocktails may reduce visual acuity as much as wearing dark glasses at night. Alcohol is not a stimulant; it is classified medically as a depressant. Coffee or other stimulants will not offset the effects of alcohol; only time can eliminate alcohol from the bloodstream. It takes at least three hours to eliminate one ounce of pure alcohol from the bloodstream.

1. Alcohol is classified by doctors as a   1.____

    A. stimulant   B. sedative
    C. depressant   D. medicine

2. Social drinkers   2.____

    A. never become obviously intoxicated
    B. always drink in large groups
    C. drive better after two cocktails
    D. are a greater menace than commonly believed

3. Alcohol will BEST be eliminated from the bloodstream by   3.____

    A. fresh air   B. a stimulant
    C. coffee   D. time

4. More than half of the fatal accidents on holiday weekends involve _____ drivers.   4.____

    A. inexperienced   B. drinking
    C. fast   D. slow

5. Drinking to any extent does NOT   5.____

    A. impair judgment
    B. decrease visual acuity
    C. reduce accident potential
    D. affect driving ability

6. In traffic accidents resulting in death, a drinking driver is involved   6.____

    A. about one-third of the time
    B. mainly at night
    C. more than 80% of the time
    D. practically all the time on weekends

7. After taking two alcoholic drinks, it is best NOT to drive until after you have   7.____

    A. had a cup of black coffee
    B. waited three hours
    C. eaten a full meal
    D. taken a half-hour nap

Questions 8-12.

DIRECTIONS: Questions 8 through 12 are to be answered ONLY on the basis of the Information contained in the following accident report.

REPORT OF ACCIDENT

Date of Accident: Nov. 27, _____ Time: 2:20 PM Date of Report: 11/28

Department Vehicle	Vehicle No. 2
Operator's Name: John Doe	Operator's Name: Richard Roe
Title: Motor Vehicle Operator	Operator's Address: 983 E. 84 St.
Vehicle Code No.: 17-129	Owner's Name: Robert Roe
License Plate No.: IN-2345	Owner's Address: 983 E. 84 St.
Damage to Vehicle: Crumpled and	License Plate No.: 9Y-8765
torn front left fender, broken	Damage to Vehicle: Crumpled right
left headlight,front bumper	front fender, broken right head-
bent outward on left side,	light and parking light, right left front
hubcap dented badly	side of front bumper badly bent
and torn off	

Place of Accident: 71st & 3rd Ave.

Description of Accident: I was driving west on 71st St. and started to turn north into 3rd Avenue since the light was still green for me. I stopped at the crosswalk because a woman was in the middle of 3rd Avenue crossing from west to east. She had just cleared my car when a Ford sedan, going north, crashed into my left front fender. The light was green on 3rd Ave. when he hit me. The woman who had crossed the avenue in front of me, and whose name I got as a witness, was standing on the corner when I got out of the car.

Persons Injured

_____   _____

_____   _____

Mrs. Mary Brown   Witness   215 E. 71 St.

Report prepared by: John Doe
Title: Motor Vehicle Operator
Badge #17832

8. According to the description of the accident, the diagram that would BEST show how and   8.____
where the vehicles crashed and the position of the witness (X) is

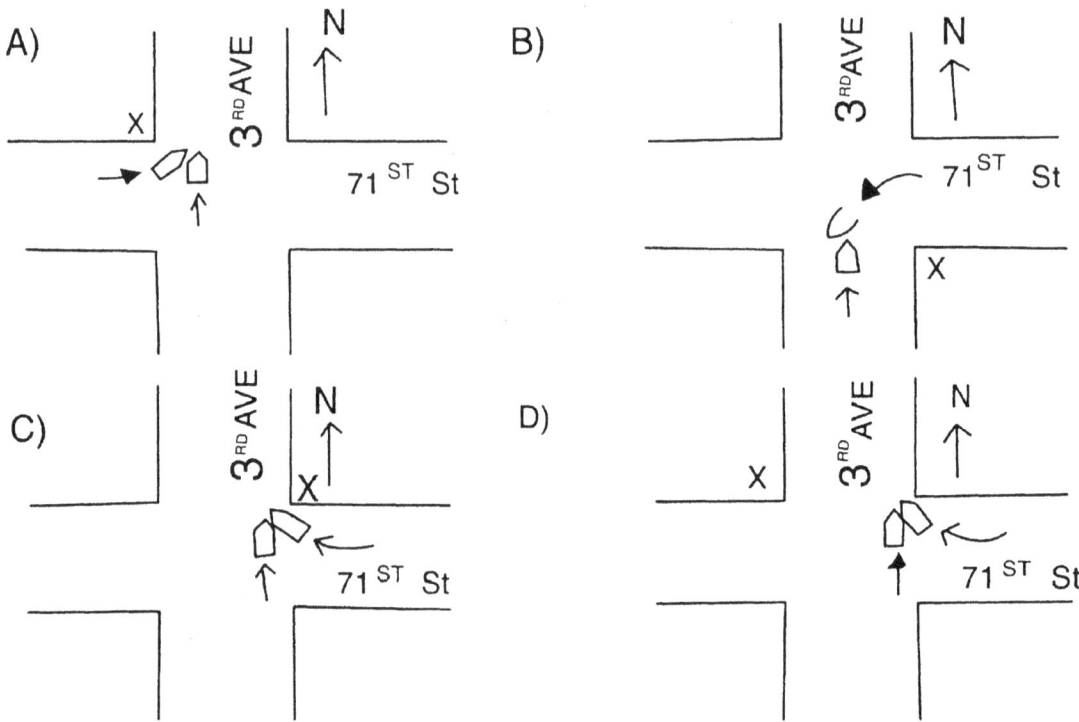

9. The pedestrian mentioned in the description of the accident was   9.____

   A. an unknown woman   B. Mary Brown
   C. an unknown man   D. Robert Roe

10. According to the information in the report, the one of the following statements which is   10.____
    INCORRECT is

   A. both cars were moving when the accident happened
   B. one car was moving when the accident happened
   C. the Department car was headed northwest when the accident happened
   D. the traffic lights had changed just before the accident happened

11. From the description of the accident as given in the report, the accident would PROBA-   11.____
    BLY be classified as

   A. premeditated   B. calamitous
   C. minor   D. fatal

12. From a reading of the accident report, it can be seen that 12.____

    A. the witness was completely unfamiliar with the neighborhood in which the accident took place
    B. the accident occurred in the early hours of the morning
    C. neither driver owned the vehicle he was driving
    D. it was raining when the accident took place

Questions 13-24.

DIRECTIONS: Questions 13 through 24 are based on the description of an automobile accident given below. Read the description carefully before answering these questions.

DESCRIPTION OF AUTOMOBILE ACCIDENT

Ten persons were injured, two critically, when a driverless auto – its accelerator jammed – ran wild through the busy intersection at 8th Ave. and 42nd Street at 11:30 A.M. yesterday. The car struck a truck, overturned it, and mounted the sidewalk. Several persons were bowled over before the car was finally stopped by collision with a second truck. Police Officer Fred Black, Badge No. 82143, said that the freak accident occurred after the car's driver, Mrs. Mary Jones, 39, of Queens, got out of the car with her daughter, Gloria, aged 3, while the engine was still running. Mr. Herbert Field, 64, of the Bronx, a passenger in the car, accidentally stepped on the accelerator when he tried to get out. This caused the car to shoot forward because the shift was in *drive*, and 5 pedestrians were thrown to the ground.

13. This accident occurred 13.____

    A. late in the morning   B. early in the morning
    C. early in the afternoon   D. ate in the evening

14. The number of persons who were injured, but not critically, is 14.____

    A. 2   B. 5   C. 8   D. 10

15. This accident occurred a block away from 15.____

    A. Grand Central Terminal   B. Times Square
    C. Union Square   D. Pennsylvania Station

16. The runaway car was finally stopped just after it 16.____

    A. mounted the sidewalk
    B. collided with a second truck
    C. crossed the intersection
    D. bowled over several persons

17. It can be inferred from the description that the driverless auto had 17.____

    A. power brakes   B. power steering
    C. a turn indicator   D. an automatic shift

18. The number on the police officer's badge is 18.____

    A. 82314   B. 82413   C. 82143   D. 82341

19. The first name of the driver of the car is   19.____

    A. Mary   B. Fred   C. Gloria   D. Herbert

20. According to the accident description, the adult passenger lives in   20.____

    A. the Bronx, and so does the driver
    B. Queens, and so does the driver
    C. the Bronx, and the driver in Queens
    D. Queens, and the driver in the Bronx

21. The number of pedestrians who were thrown to the ground is   21.____

    A. 2   B. 5   C. 7   D. 10

22. The person who made a statement about the runaway car was   22.____

    A. Herbert Field   B. Mary Jones
    C. Gloria Jones   D. Fred Black

23. Herbert Field is older than Mary Jones by about _____ years.   23.____

    A. 25   B. 35   C. 51   D. 61

24. The car shot forward immediately after   24.____

    A. Mrs. Jones placed the shift in *drive*
    B. Mr. Field stepped on the accelerator
    C. Mrs. Jones stepped out of the car
    D. Mr. Field got out of the car

Questions 25-28.

DIRECTIONS: Questions 25 through 28 are to be answered ONLY on the basis of the information given in the following passage.

ACCIDENT PRONENESS

Accident proneness is a subject deserving much more attention than it has received. Studies have shown a high incidence of accidents to be associated with particular employees who are called accident prone. Such employees, according to these studies, behave on their jobs in ways which make them likely to have more accidents than would normally be expected.

It is important to point out the difference between the employee who is a *repeater* and the one who is truly accident prone. It is obvious that any person assigned to work about which he knows little will be liable to injury until he does learn the *how* of the job. Few workers left completely on their own will develop adequate safe practices. Therefore, they must be trained. Only those who fail to respond to proper training should be regarded as accident prone.

The dangers of an occupation should also be considered when judging an accident record. For a crane operator, a record of five accidents in a given period of time may not indicate accident proneness, while, in the case of a clerk, two accidents over the same period of time may be excessive. There are the reporters whose accident records can be explained by correctible physical defects, by correctible unsafe plant or machine conditions, or by assignment to work for which they are not suited because they cannot meet all the job's physical requirements. Such repeaters cannot be fairly called *accident prone*. A diagnosis of accident proneness should not be lightly made but should be based on all of these considerations.

25. According to the above passage, studies have shown that accident prone employees   25.____

    A.   work under unsafe physical conditions
    B.   act in unsafe ways on the job
    C.   are not usually physically suited for their jobs
    D.   work in the more dangerous occupations

26. According to the above passage, a person who is accident prone   26.____

    A.   has received proper training which has not reduced his tendency toward accidents
    B.   repeats the same accident several times over a short period of time
    C.   experiences excessive anxiety about dangers in his occupation
    D.   ignores unsafe but correctible machine conditions

27. According to the above passage, MOST persons who are given work they know little about   27.____

    A.   will eventually learn on their own sufficient safety practices to follow
    B.   work safely if they are not accident prone
    C.   must be trained before they develop adequate safety methods
    D.   should be regarded as accident prone until they become familiar with the job

28. According to the above passage, to effectively judge the accident record of an employee, one should consider   28.____

    A.   the employee's age and physical condition
    B.   that five accidents are excessive
    C.   the type of dangers that are natural to his job
    D.   the difficulty level of previous occupations held by the employee

Questions 29-30.

DIRECTIONS: Questions 29 and 30 are to be answered ONLY on the basis of the information given in the following paragraph.

When heavy rain beats on your windshield, it becomes hard for you to see ahead and even harder to see objects to the side — despite good windshield wipers. Also, the danger zone becomes longer when it is raining because the car takes longer to stop on wet streets. Remember that the danger zone of your car is the distance within which you can't stop after you have seen something on the road ahead of your car. The way to reduce the length of the danger zone of your car while driving is to reduce speed.

29. From the information in the above paragraph, you cannot tell if the danger zone of your car   29._____

    A. can be made smaller
    B. is greater on a rainy day
    C. is greater on cloudy days than on clear days
    D. is the distance in back of the car or in front of the car

30. According to the above paragraph, the danger zone of a moving car is affected by   30._____

    A. the condition of the street and the speed of the car
    B. many things which cannot be pinned down, in addition to the mechanical condition of the car
    C. the number of objects to the front and to the side
    D. visibility of the road and the reaction time of the driver

---

KEY (CORRECT ANSWERS)

1.	C	16.	B
2.	D	17.	D
3.	D	18.	C
4.	B	19.	A
5.	C	20.	C
6.	A	21.	B
7.	B	22.	D
8.	C	23.	A
9.	B	24.	B
10.	A	25.	B
11.	C	26.	A
12.	C	27.	C
13.	A	28.	C
14.	C	29.	C
15.	B	30.	A

CPSIA information can be obtained
at www.ICGtesting.com
Printed in the USA
LVHW022054171219
640814LV00022B/505